SECRET FIGHTING ARTS
OF THE WORLD

SECRET FIGHTING ARTS OF THE WORLD

JOHN F. GILBEY

PAN BOOKS LTD
LONDON AND SYDNEY

First published 1963 by the Charles E. Tuttle Co Inc
This edition published 1974 by Pan Books Ltd,
Cavaye Place, London SW10 9PG
ISBN 0 330 24235 0
© The Charles E. Tuttle Co Inc 1963

*Printed in Great Britain by
Richard Clay (The Chaucer Press), Ltd, Bungay, Suffolk*

DEDICATION

To all those who achieved it by the highest
technique of all, that of no sweat! Let them
remember G. J. Nathan's words: 'The confidence
of amateurs is the envy of professionals.'

CONTENTS

IN PLACE OF A
FOREWORD

*'The struggling for knowledge hath a pleasure in it like
that of wrestling with a fine woman'* – G. S. Halifax

ABBE SIEYES, when asked what he did during the
French Revolution, responded: 'I survived.'

From a very early age I started a study of survival. I
think it must have been even before I learned that girls
were different from boys. It continues today. It has
gone through the very specialized arts which have
come to public popularity lately into secret personalized realms.

For I found out early that the least known is not invariably the lesser. This knowledge came first one
afternoon when I was fourteen. I was with two men
each about ten years my senior and we were walking
through the public park heading for lunch. These two
were the best street fighters in the burg: the argument
never was who could beat them – for nobody could –
but rather which of them was the best. We never
learned and both were gobbled up by time, war, and
distance.

I don't remember why I happened to be with them
(for this was something of an honour for a boy) unless
it was because I carried the money for lunch. At any
rate, halfway through the park we chanced across a
coloured man, the years crowding him, slouched
against a tree and contentedly puffing his pipe.

These boys were ornery and hungry. This combination plus that target was too much. Preceding me, without saying a word, they converged on the old man. He went on puffing. Suddenly both struck him at the same time, full on both sides of the face. Then they chuckled and stepped back to let him disintegrate. But . . . no body fell.

The old man took his pipe from his mouth, tapped the tobacco out of it, put it in his upper pocket, and said lackadaisically: 'You boys 'pear to be lookin' for trouble.'

Here was a chance for one of them to become champion: simply by staying. But neither wanted it that bad. Both went away from there fast. I – who might be considered an accessory – preceded them (I was younger and more fully committed to the doctrine: 'One pair of heels is worth two pair of hands'.).

On reflection, I think the old man was even more skilled in not having to show his skill. He illustrated the highest principle of fighting, that of not having to fight. His defence was enough to send the terrorized miscreants out of the area on the double. Anyhow, I admired him for it as I have admired others since. My research into unarmed fighting methods started that day.

It has taken me through the more popular sports of Western boxing and wrestling and into judo, *aikido*, *karate*, and Chinese boxing. These forms are currently gaining world popularity and are thus fairly familiar to most people. But what of the more secret personalized methods which are not included in the more popular schools? Who is to say something for them? Indeed, who can?

In studying the more orthodox methods I have encountered famous masters capable of monstrous misbehaviour with highly personalized tools of destruction. Through cajolery, begging, borrowing, and sheer thievery I have learned as much about these esoteric systems as any living man. The Publisher has persuaded me to present them here for the reader's study and elucidation.

Two notes before we jump in. One: all of these methods are dangerous, terribly so. Men were actually killed in perfecting many of them. Therefore, be careful! When practising with a friend, work for speed and placement. Save your power for the heavy bag and other auxiliary equipment. Two: I am no Faulkner. The stories I tell here rest squarely on memory and notes, both of which are subject to human frailty. I have omitted inessential details and cut out all the gingerbread I might have used to dramatize the situations. For the drama was in the action and words of the masters and I desired nothing to detract from them.

I think the reader can derive a philosophy of fighting from this volume. I know he can learn tactics. He should study hard and make these techniques his own. Surely then his life will be enriched. Mine was.

September, 1962
John F. Gilbey
Reykjavik, Iceland

1
THE DELAYED
DEATH TOUCH

'A fatal blow impress'd the Seal of Death'
P. *Whitehead*

I HAD heard for years of the delayed death touch.
Various Japanese, Korean and Chinese sources con-
tended that they had seen it. On the face of it, it
sounded preposterous. Sure, a well-concentrated and
well-placed *atemi* (strike) could make a man shuffle off
this mortal coil – this is demonstrable. But to ask a man
to believe that a light touch which could go almost un-
noticed by the victim could lead two weeks or two
months later to the onset of serious internal disturb-
ances often resulting in death was asking too much. I
was not prepared to believe it even after seeing many
incredible feats in combatives down through the years.

After some time in *karate* gyms in Asia, never once
even getting close to a demonstration of this power, I
journeyed in 1955 to Taiwan. There I saw gifted boxers
of every description. Men who could slice bricks like
your wife would a cake; men who could lightly touch
your body and bring a bright red blood line immediately to the surface; men who could support over
a two-hundred-pound weight attached to their genitalia; men who could catch flies (alive!) with their
chopsticks; men who could plunge their arms up to the
elbow in unprepared, rather hard soil; and men who

set fire to their fingers. But it was not given me to see the delayed death touch, and in 1957 I prepared to de-camp.

A week before my ship was scheduled to leave, I in-terviewed a famous Taiwanese *shaolin* teacher, Oh Hsin-yang, in the capital. His demonstrations of the boxing art were at once beautiful and powerful. And his conversation was effervescent (his command of Mandarin was sure enough for us to dispose of an in-terpreter). With appropriate anatomical charts he explained that *shaolin* masters for centuries had been guided in their *atemi* by the time of day. The blood, he said, comes close to the surface at different times during the day. A boxer had only to be aware of the course of this circulation and to attack the appropriate part at the time the blood was near the surface. Injury was certain and death probable then.

The method, he went on, was time tested and sure. Any number of doctors of traditional Chinese medicine could attest to its truth. Indeed, if the victim of a fight came (or more likely, were brought) to a doctor, the doctor could expedite the treatment by consulting the body charts. For invariably in those cases where experts had been involved, the injury had resulted from such a time strike.

This was astounding. There was nothing to rival it in the West. But still, I had only his word for it. Would it work? Could I see some proof?

At this request Oh's small beard fairly bristled but his countenance changed not a whit. I hurriedly gushed out that while I was prepared to believe his remarks without requiring proof, there were many sceptics in the West who would not. They would be convinced only after some sort of tangible demonstration.

He cut my drivel short by barking a command and

from the rear of the room a youngster of about twenty-five, stolid and smooth-muscled, came forward. Oh rose from his stool and approached his student. Without any preliminaries Oh struck him swiftly though not too powerfully on the left external obliques. A small red mark was visibly evident immediately – this leads me to believe that the punch was a knuckle(s)-focused one and not a full-fisted attack.

Oh resumed his seat and the student tottered to a couch and crumpled on to it with the assistance of two other men. Oh commented that since it would be far too dangerous at that time (nearly 3 PM) to attack a high blood organ, he had done the next best thing – he had purposely missed his target, getting close enough only to demonstrate minimal effects of the method.

He took my elbow and propelled me to the couch. The youth was lying on his back: his entire body reminded me of a wet rag. His eyes were open but not focused, staring. His breathing was stertorous and hurried. I felt his forehead and was not surprised to find it almost cold and quite clammy.

Oh said, 'You cannot believe that he could fight a moment more.'

I answered, 'No, I believe he could not.'

'Yet,' Oh went on, 'how do you scientists of the West explain it? I struck him lightly at a point much buffeted in Western boxing contests. In those contests a punch such as mine would have not only not disturbed my antagonist but would have also left me open for his counter. You must believe that skill and strength are not the only requisites in fighting. Knowledge of where to hit is also important. You, of course, realized that before today. But today you learned an equally important thing – when to hit. Our fate is not only in the stars but also in the hours. Remember that.'

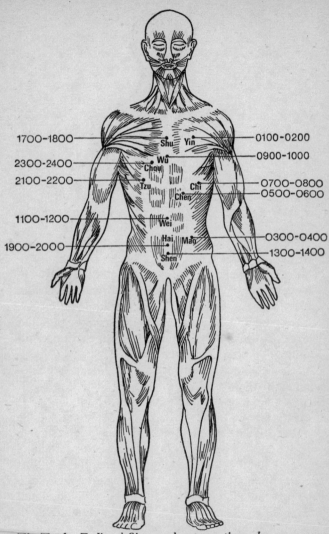

1700–1800
2300–2400
2100–2200
1100–1200
1900–2000

0100–0200
0900–1000
0700–0800
0500–0600
0300–0400
1300–1400

Shu   Yin
Wu
Chou
Tzu
Chi
Chen
Wei
Hai   Mao
Shen

The Twelve Zodiacal Signs each representing a human organ equated to a specific time when an attack to that organ is most critical. English equivalents for Chinese terms: Yin – Lungs; Shu – Upper Heart; Wu – Heart; Chou – Liver; Tzu –

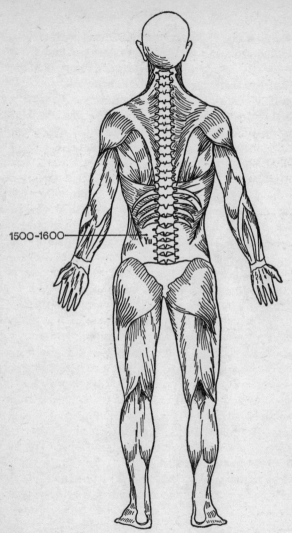

1500-1600 ——— Yu

Bile; Chen – Stomach; Wei – Small Intestine; Mao – Large
Intestine; Hai – Navel; Shen – Bladder; Szu – Spleen; Yu –
Kidney

By now the youth was being administered medicine of some kind and his breathing was becoming more regular. To my question as to his condition, Oh responded that the medicine would bring him round but that he would not box for a month or so. Thus the internal environment would have time to correct and heal.

I was tired and a bit upset. After the demonstration our conversation flagged and I prepared to leave. Suddenly though, I remembered the delayed death touch. Was the time strike a manifestation of the same power? Disregarding compunctions about taking more of his time after several hours freely given, I asked him. Had he ever heard of it?

He didn't answer right off. He looked quietly at me. This continued for a minute or more. I kept my eyes on his while my heart raged within me and my reason told me I had gone too far – I had insulted him.

He spoke some words in Taiwanese which I didn't understand and the youth, couch and all, was carried out. The others left with him except for one young boy, perhaps fifteen or so. Then Oh turned to me.

'Your tone,' he started, 'implies that you equate this so-called delayed death touch with the time strike you just witnessed. You are correct. However, the ability to perform such a feat is quite beyond most masters, even the highest. On Taiwan I alone possess this ability. But I seldom show this skill even' – and I winced – 'for Chinese.'

At this juncture he smiled for the first time that day and said, 'For one thing, the control is somewhat less sure than in a simple time strike. Therefore, the danger is greater. Subjects are harder to come by. Who would submit to such a touch where the danger is not only physical but psychic as well? Not very many I fear. Would you?'

I didn't answer immediately, feeling he was being jocose and would move on in his recitation. But he didn't. He sat there with that maddening faint smile and waited. And waited.

Then my words came as out of a bucket. I was unqualified. I was not even a boxer. My age was against it. My ship was leaving in a week. And so on.

He belly-laughed at this, put his hand up to signal me to silence, and only then did I realize that he *had* been joking.

He pointed at the boy in the rear of the room and the youth unhesitatingly came forward. 'My son has never had the experience and needs it badly,' he said simply.

I stood up and watched intently. Oh gesticulated with his right index finger and put it lightly on a point just below his son's navel. Then he turned again to me.

'That is all, just a touch, the *ch'i* [inner air or energy] transmitted very smoothly. Since you leave in a week I have timed the effect of this touch for three days hence. About noon on that day Ah-lin will begin to vomit and must go to bed. So that your Western cohorts will not accuse me of chicanery I make you a present of Ah-lin until that time. I shall meet you in Taipei three days hence at the Union Hotel. Until then, farewell.'

Thus our conversation ended. Ah-lin with his perpetual smile and his light step returned with me to Taipei. When I asked him if he had felt his father's touch he replied negatively. The next three days we were inseparable and I grew quite fond of him. He was most helpful and even aided in packing my freight for shipment.

On the morning of the third day Mr Oh came to my hotel attired in a Western business suit. After the usual formalities and while we were drinking tea he asked me whether I had kept vigilance over Ah-lin. I told him soberly that the boy had not been out of my sight.

The three of us took a brisk stroll through the disordered, squalid downtown area of the city and repaired to the hotel just as the clock hands were coinciding straight up. We went to my room where the father and I sat on the only two chairs and Ah-lin reclined on the bed. We chit-chatted with animation but my mind was on only one thing – the time. Discreetly I looked at my wristwatch (12.05 PM) and the old man saw the movement.

'Don't worry,' he mused, 'the thing will happen. And I had better prepare.'

So saying, he broke open a small satchel he had brought with him and took from it several bottles of various-coloured liquids. He took them into the adjoining bathroom and busied himself for perhaps five minutes. Returning, he sat down again in the chair furthest away from the bed.

No more than three or four minutes had elapsed when Ah-lin somewhat self-consciously spoke out to break the silence.

'So far, Father, absolutely noth . . .' his voice trailed off there and stopped.

Oh stood up and said crisply, 'It's happened,' walked to the bed and felt the pulse of his now unconscious son. In another minute he was in the bathroom opening bottles and stirring a mixture of the assorted liquids.

I walked to the bed and felt an almost undetectable pulse. This, along with the open, vacant eyes frightened me. I returned to my chair. I felt utterly helpless sitting there and Oh paid me no mind. Soon he was ministering to the boy who quickly sat up, conscious, then lay back with an anguished sigh. He drank some of the medicine, and some of the chalkiness of his pallor disappeared. After some massage, alternate hot and cold compresses, and more medicine, Ah-lin began to look himself.

Only then did Oh turn to me. He made no pretence of hiding a look of supreme tiredness. Nor was his voice quite so kind as before. It was as though he had been dared, had performed – almost at the risk of his son's life – and now wished I'd get the hell out of there.

'You have seen,' he said simply.

'Will the boy be all right?' I asked anxiously.

Wearily he said, 'Yes, there is nothing to fear – he is coming round. But it was touch and go for a time. The balance was frightfully close. But that was my problem. It's all right now. Ah-lin will convalesce for three months and will have no after-effects.'

And then, 'Were you satisfied?'

I was, I told him. I thanked him and somewhat ashamedly departed. I felt like I had done something dirty to a boy to whom I had grown quite attached.

But the test had been most successful. I had seen the delayed death touch. It had – unfortunately – almost resulted in the designed end. I could verify that it existed and do homage to Oh Hsin-yang, its master, at the same time. Even with the satisfaction this knowledge brought, I dragged through the last few days. But on the final day, as my boat pulled out, my dark mood lifted when from the deck I saw a smiling Ah-lin and his father sprint on to the pier from a pedicab. They stood waving until the ship was well away from the pier and their figures were indistinguishable. I think they knew my feelings and came to erase them. They succeeded.

2
THE LIVERPOOL NUTTER

'There are two things an Englishman understands, hard words and hard blows' – W. Hazlitt

LIVERPOOL is a port. And ports are tough cities. Not as tough as most writers make them, but still tough.

I had worked out at judo in a dirty little dojo in a dirty little street and had repaired to a small grog-shop with a few of the boys. We talked of judo for an endless time (we 'tired the moon with our talking' in that fine W. H. Hudson phrase).

A wiry figure of a man strutted in as if he owned the place, brooking no impediment. I nodded towards him.

'Who's the cocky bird?' I asked of no one in particular.

The boys looked up and one, Jim Onions, said: 'That's Ian Lindsey. He's a crackin' tough one I can tell you.'

This spurred my interest. How did he mean 'tough' – was he a judo man? I asked.

Onions responded: 'Not this one. Strictly street stuff, him. And good at it too. I've seen him in a couple of goes and he keeps 'em brief. He uses his head.'

At this, the others laughed as at a pun. Searching for meaning in this sudden laughter I observed that any man who didn't use his head in the street didn't last long.

'No, no,' Onions laughed, 'I meant he really uses his head, his nut, as we say. Lindsey is a nutter, probably the best around. I don't know any that're better.'

Of course he had me then. I plied him with further questions about Lindsey while I thought of the head-men I had known. In Korea you would expect the head tactic to reach a high science since most street fights resemble a contest of mountain goats. But it doesn't. In China I had known one famous boxer, Lu An-to, who pounded large nails into two-by-fours with his fore-head and yanked them out, still perfectly straight, with his teeth. And yet other boxers depreciated this man who – in Chesterton's phrase – 'had a head you could break doors with'. They claimed that his head art was 'all right' but it was all he could do (they may have overlooked the fact that he yanked the nails out – I would hate to have my ear within those incisors!).

I told Onions that I simply had to talk with Lindsey. Onions laughed again, saying that it would be no problem. Lindsey would talk all night as long as his beer glass was kept full. Onions then went to the bar and spoke to Lindsey who looked back at our table several times during Onions' pitch. Finally he accom-panied Onions back to the table and took a chair next to me. After the appropriate formalities, I asked Lind-sey about his head tactic.

Through thin lips his Scouse voice told me these things about nutting. He considered it a science though most people felt it was crude and limited as an offen-sive method. They hadn't put the required energy into its practice; thus they didn't know – couldn't know. Others, when they used the nut, used it incorrectly. Some even charged, attempting to butt with the head into their antagonist's breadbasket. This tactic was so amateurish as to be beneath mention.

Above all, nutting required industry, practice. Lindsey said he had practised it a minimum of one hour daily for twenty years. He considered it close combat *par excellence*. In over one hundred combats, sometimes

Ian Lindsey's Nut

even opposed by two men simultaneously, this tactic had allowed him to emerge victorious.

Then he stood up and, using Onions as an opponent, continued alternately talking and demonstrating. For practice he used a firmly packed head-sized sandbag placed atop a larger sandbag. A scarf was tied between the two. His approach was essentially frontal or from the sides (since it is practically impossible to get behind a man without contact), although the rear nut was effective also. After coming into range, he would grasp the scarf, and, while pulling the simulated head forward, he would thrust his forehead in a rapid-fire staccato against the front surface of the head. The sequence involved at least seven hits, the focus being on the nose, the under-nose area, and the temples. (Here he did not hit Onions, only approaching him and nutting the air.)

Nor was the attack arbitrary. Each hit was designed to hit where it invariably hit, each carried full power, and yet all seven were so quickly delivered (under a second for the full sequence according to my stop-watch when I timed him the next day) that the eye could not differentiate them on an individual basis.

The scarf which simulated an opponent's lapels was not indispensable. Lindsey would often use one hand or both in a rapid circular motion to bring his enemy's head into the impact area. To get close enough he would vary his tactics, sometimes fighting into a lock-up position, or often playing the innocent and talking his way in close and there launching his attack.

The entire ridge of the head was used, but never the top of the head. I told him of a Chinese boxer who used the top as the attacking element and could even break bricks and tiles with it. He said that this was unusual and he could not recommend it for the average man. It was his view also to avoid the mouth area, since the opponent's teeth could often harm the attacker more than the attacked. Another safety reminder was to attach the tip of the tongue to the roof of the mouth so that you didn't bite your own tongue during the attack.

Was it true, I asked him, that some nutters even sewed a razor blade into their caps, thus giving an even greater poignancy to the onslaught? He snorted at this. Only amateurs who knew little of nutting ever resorted to such tricks, he said. I said that this was the same observation Chinese made regarding those boxers who sewed razor-sharp coins into the sides of their shoes so as to increase their kicking artistry.

I never saw Lindsey in actual combat. I didn't have to. He had shown enough for me to mark him down as the greatest 'headhunter' I had ever seen.

3
FIST FIGHTERS
OF BENARES

'Whatsoever thy hand findeth to do, do it with thy might'
Ecclesiastes 9:10

SHAOLIN boxers may laugh at the present day antics of *karate* men in Okinawa, Korea, and Japan, but to a man they revere and respect the traditional fist fighting of India. After all this is where *shaolin* originated and you don't – or shouldn't – criticize your antecedents.

Most Westerners think of India as a former British colony made up of scrawny mendicants. Some few, however, know that on its wrestling prowess alone India stands high as an athletic country. Gama didn't come out of Dubuque. But almost no one knows that striking as well as grappling is an Indian forte. For fist fighting is not publicized. It is kept in the utmost secrecy.

Time was when annual competitions of fisticuffs were held in Benares. This would take the form of both individual and group battles. The contestants hardened their fists to a condition in which coconuts and stones could be smashed with one blow. Since, unlike *karate*, these battles featured contact, violence was inevitable. Deaths ensued and the police banned such meetings.

In 1952 I arrived in Benares, no Shangri-La for looks, but then no Calcutta either. I spoke to University professors, Sikh taxi drivers, warehousemen, waiters, and a desk clerk at the YMCA. Did they know where I could find a boxing teacher? Negative response all around.

But one day I was having dinner with a Britisher, D. Rodgers, *bon vivant*, an affluent manager of a metallurgical concern. Rodgers liked Western boxing and we discussed it often. This day he was deploring Britain's inability to offer anything but Scotts and Cockells to the sport. This started us off on the question of why certain nations rise and fall in boxing during certain periods. Britain was supreme through the eighteenth century, then France had her brief heyday which ended with Carpentier's failure before Dempsey, then the US had taken over. Even in the US various nationalities monopolized the titles during certain periods. The Irish, Italians, Jews and Negroes had all had their day of glory. Why was that day so short and why did such a different crowd arrive?

We were at the coffee and brandy and the issue was like a greased pig – difficult of purchase. About then, I asked why it was that India had never taken to boxing. Rodgers answered that the Indians believed that putting a glove over a fist was sacrilege; it defiled nature. Nature insisted that the fist when it needed to strike be unhampered by cushions.

Did he mean that the Indians had a traditional boxing sport? (I knew but played it straight; at this juncture Rodgers seemed knowledgeable enough for me to learn.) They did, he responded, a corking good one too. The art, he continued, was unfortunately dying. Police intervention restricted competitions and this was drying up the wellsprings of the art. The few remaining teachers, moreover, refused to promote the art among foreigners (as the Japanese were doing with *karate*). To them it was almost a religious observance, not to be taken lightly.

I observed that he seemed to know a lot about it. If it were so secret, how came he to this knowledge? He chuckled and in an *entre nous* tone informed me that the greatest fistic master in Benares, in India, in the World (!), a foundry shop foreman at his plant, had been teaching him twice a week for five years.

It only remained then to tell Rodgers of my research and my deep interest. The next night we were in the home of his master, Dunraj Seth, in the suburbs. At first the master was not prepossessing: he was about 5′ 8″, 180 pounds, and he had a modest pot beginning on his middle. But he looked canny and willing.

At the introduction I was mouthing the unctuous phrases so welcome to the ears of Asians. He interrupted me by saying in perfect English, 'Hitting is not important, but hitting and hurting is. For example, sir, a splendid time to hit a man in the mouth is while he is talking!'

At this I flushed and sat down while Seth continued.

'Another excellent opportunity is when a man is eating or smoking. In short, any time when he is not set for it. I am not saying that a human head can absorb a fist strike with impunity. Your Max Baer trained for a match by letting friends hit him in the head and only desisted when he started walking in circles and hearing non-existent bells. But you *can* set the head and by manoeuvring it mitigate the punches of even a skilled opponent. And if the opponent is unskilled, a master can resist his strike. Please stand.'

I stood, uncertain.

'I want you to hit me with all your strength anywhere on my head. Do not be afraid for me. I know of your background. Both Chinese and Japanese boxers

Although Seth's Long Attack is powerful, it must be combined with short tactics or it will be blocked

have had their turns. It is now yours. If, however, I feel that you are pulling your punch out of deference for me, our interview will end there.'

What could I do? He had set the frame of reference succinctly. I looked hastily at Rodgers for support but he only smiled softly. So I retracted my right fist in the accepted *karate* forward stance (*zenkutsu-dachi*) and, with a *kiai*-shout, shot my right fore-fist (*seiken*) flush into his mouth.

His mien didn't change. He looked at me with humour in his eyes.

'You have fair power, sir. Please sit down and we'll continue our discussion.'

Incredulously, I resumed my seat and listened in wonder to this fistic marvel.

'We began that way because that is the way I began and the way my students start. To attack, one must be capable of defending. And the ability to withstand a full punch is part of defending. It takes several years, however, and is not learned overnight. Otherwise we would have experienced the same results as Mr Baer.'

Holding up a gnarled, beefy fist, he continued.

'This is the fist, the weapon, the tool. It must be clenched tightly. Now you have your weapon. How do you use it? We use it in two ways. First in the more or less ordinary way, as an extension of the body, specifically the arm. But there is another way. The fist can be submerged into the arm in such a way that it is only the point of the spear, so to speak. Here the arm, not the fist, is the weapon. In this type of attack the arm is rigidly straight and not bent at the elbow. The power generated in this "long" attack is truly enormous but, as you can well guess, this must be meshed with a short attack or it is fairly easy to defend.

'Now, when you strike it must not be haphazard. Every hit must have a target, and every target, a reason. Generally the temples, throat, solar plexus and groin are the best targets, for an effective hit in any of these places is often fatal.

'I do not stress kicking. There are many good methods. But there are only twenty-four hours in a day. If I could kick I would be an imperfect boxer. And in all humility I tell you my boxing is not imperfect.'

He took us into the next room where two superbly conditioned athletes were doing *baitaks* (deep squats). The room was dimly lighted but airily ventilated, opening on to a small courtyard. It was somewhat larger than the living room; it probably measured twenty by thirty-five feet.

'This,' he said, sweeping an arm across the room, 'is our gym and these are my pupils. Save for Mr Rodgers, my only pupils. Traditional fist fighting is kept secret, very secret, in India. The reason we do not popularize it is because we fear abuse. Not only from its religious aspect but also from the physical. These two fighters are my sons; our family has had boxers in every generation for centuries. We limit instruction because we wish it to retain its religious and family flavour and because if it is misused it can kill so easily.

'One of your presidents, Thomas Jefferson, said that everyone should give two hours daily *at a minimum* to physical exercise. For fifty years I have averaged four and these boys do five – being young, their vitality is, of course, of a higher order. The practice must be regular and it must be intensive. Extensive, no. One technique mastered is worth one thousand sampled. We stress few and we stress repetitions.'

He spoke quietly to his sons and they walked to a small platform against the wall. It was then I noticed that a one-inch-thick steel plate had been riveted to the wall, which itself was of poured concrete. I gaped as the first boy on the platform hit the plate with what appeared to be full power with his right hand. Then his left; and again, his right. The strikes became a staccato of sound. Now the other boy was hitting the plate. I checked their legs. It was incredible – they were not holding back. Each punch was being focused by the whole body from the soles of the feet up.

Seth noted my astonishment.

'This full power punch on steel they also come to gradually. The bones of the hand must be formed, not deformed, and this can only be done slowly. Can your

Japanese or Chinese do this? I think not. In fact the *karate makiwara* (punching post) is so resilient at the striking point that you hardly need to hit it to make it move. I aver that that is too easy – it doesn't let a man develop.

'These boys will strike the steel for one hour, varying the pattern so that the fists are not used alternately throughout. Often they will use their lefts three times in succession followed by their rights twice in succession, and so on. The reason for this is too obvious to require explanation.

'What you are seeing is only the outward manifestation of the punches. The intricate niceties are the heart of the method and are fairly complex. Too complex to pass on to you now. Perhaps on your next visit . . .? Generally, let me say that as the target is not arbitrary, neither is the technique. The entire body – external and internal – must be incorporated into each punch. Then and only then can it have a meaningful impact. The externals, the forming of the fist, the posture, the shifting of weight, and so on, take time but they are relatively easy to assimilate. The internals, the breathing, the focus of energy (your Chinese call this *ch'i*, I believe) take decades and at least twice as long is spent daily in their practice than on the mere hitting.'

Turning his back on me he walked into the living room saying (almost over his shoulder), 'I think that is enough.' And that ended our discussion. I was able to get a bit more about the system from Rodgers. It too was impressive. Seth did not, Rodgers told me, teach long involved forms (*kata*). He taught only short sequences. Nor did he believe in a flurry of punches. One punch properly focused and delivered he believed was worth a hundred merely tossed into an antagonist. A real first class master, this one!

* * *

Rodgers also took me to see Seth's cousin who had a small boxing school in the eastern section. This school was somewhat more commercial than Seth's but even more specialized. This teacher taught a system which made almost sole use of the thumbs. I learned that thumbs can be used other places than on a butcher's

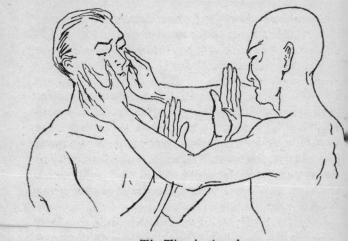

The Thumb Attack

scales. The eyes and the junctures of muscle groups were the targets and this teacher was a marvel at forking his thumbs in where he wanted them with incredible swiftness. The teacher's fists and knees were likewise employed, albeit sparingly.

One technique I found especially good. Since space is a great defeater of placement it is always best to channel your strike on something substantial. The Chinese, for example, prefer to hit only when they can guide their punch along either their or their opponent's arm. This thumb artist would slide either or both of his open hands, thumbs extended, along either side of an opponent's head. The extended thumbs would easily guide into his eyes. You couldn't miss with this.

The system was effective, I felt, and I was especially moved by the formalism used. Everything was very ritualized. For example, the class opened and closed with the mass recitation of the Credo, which went:

> I come to you with only thumbs,
> Other weapons I have not.
> But should Right or Honour require it
> My thumbs will bear me out.

For some reason this recitation always had a great impact on me. The teacher and students took it very seriously; the moment was always a sober one. Here were these athletes with these very dangerous weapons pleading for peace but, if that didn't avail, warning of the weapons to be used. Each time I heard it I found a feeling I hadn't encountered for years: that of being close to tears.

Even Rodgers's humorous asterisk to the Credo 'and if my thumbs don't kill, my knees will' didn't snap me out of the sober mood induced by it. Only now from the vantage point of time and distance can I view it dispassionately.

4
GANGES GROIN GOUGE

'He was not a sweet-tempered man, nor one of gentlemood'
Homer

SRIM BABA is a nut-brown coloured man, one chin too many, who fears no one and has nothing to fear. He lives along the Ganges not far from Benares.

Baba is a specialist and a real good one. His speciality is to attack in diverse ways that which is called in China 'the golden target' and in America, 'the family jewels'. His art is so secret that he is not famous except among the top boxers of India, but, believe me, this is recommendation enough. He hides his art and has but one student.

It took two years of letters, gifts, influence and pressure to bring about a meeting between us. But when we finally came together it was an electric four hours and worth all the trouble it took.

In those four hours Srim never once looked directly at me. He made no attempt to hide his dislike of me and his disapproval of the interview. Frankly, he had been forced into it by various means and he wasn't liking it. However, it was no less professional a presentation than if he had enjoyed it.

We were alone and he began in impeccable English: 'The groin is my target. The strongest man in the world becomes weak as a child when struck there.* Once struck, there is no defence against subsequent attack. Moreover, the striking need not be hard nor squarely on target. A quick, light slap partially deflected but still landing on a portion of the privates has nearly the same effect as a strong, square strike.

'You may ask, if this is true – if just a slight slap which barely hits the target will suffice – why then make such a fetish of studying it properly? Simply because the target is mobile and not at all easy to hit. By studying it precisely we may hope to penetrate our antagonist. Without a method, you could never hope to hit even a mediocre boxer in this place.

'But with a method and with practice, expert boxers will fall before you. I learned that from a teacher who spent forty years creating and delineating it. I have practised it forty-five years, perfecting the secrets he taught me. Thus the method is almost a century old, known to only three persons, and shown' – and here he looked in my direction resentfully – 'to one.

'The first thing is the approach. This can be done from any direction; however, from the side the target is somewhat harder to hit. Next, the posture. You may stand high, middle, or low; stiff-bodied or relaxed. It is well to vary these postures and attitudes; otherwise your opponent can construct an appropriate offence and defence against you.

'Next, the actual strike. This may be done with hand,

---

* The classic story on this concerns the rich dowagers standing in a garden discussing the worst pain in the world. One thought that a toothache or earache was the worst; another opined that no pain was equal to that of childbirth; another mentioned migraine. At this point the gardener, overhearing the context, could not be constrained and broke in with: 'Say, any you ladies ever been kicked in the scrotum?'

foot, elbow, or knee, and may be part of a straight offensive sequence – in which the other strikes would have as their aim the diverting of his defence away from the ultimate target – or of a defensive counter. Thus you see it is a drastic weapon with but few if any restrictions on its use.'

He demonstrated in brisk, light movements as he talked.

'Now I have given you the target, the approach, and the *when*. Let us now look at the actual *how*. Before they are of much use in application, the hand and foot weapons must be assiduously trained. These weapons must have intrinsic power. Here, let me show you. . .'

We walked out into the alley next to which a new house was under construction. He asked me to select five bricks from one of many piles. I did. After paying the watchman a pittance for these, we returned to the room. He asked me to stack these up five-high, which I did.

'By intrinsic power,' he continued, 'I mean the power to touch with your hands and transmit instantly an injurious force. Watch.'

He then inhaled slightly, gestured with his hands, his elbows high, and, after two passes over the stack of bricks, he brought his right hand down easily and lightly on the top of the pile. He then turned his back on the pile and on me. I took this as an invitation to investigate the bricks.

I remember I was very disappointed to see the top brick completely intact.

'Would you try again?' I said to the back of his head. 'It doesn't seem to have worked.'

He sighed deeply and said in a tone of deep annoyance: 'Please look at each brick this time.'

I returned to the stack and lifted the top brick. It was

unbroken. I lifted the second brick and looked at it – it was intact. Then I looked down at the third brick, the middle of the stack, and I was flabbergasted. It not only was broken clear through its dimensions, but parts of it had crumbled almost to powder. I took a piece of it, squeezed it lightly, and it crumbled. Bricks four and five I then inspected and found intact.

By now he had resumed his seat and was beginning to speak. Hurriedly I returned to my seat, thrilled by his demonstration.

'This is not a circus stunt. No one else can do it. If your thinking is acute you will see that both force and focus were applied lightly here, so lightly in fact that the two bricks insulating the target from below and above were left undisturbed. When I attack the groin it is with the same principle pervading, regardless of which technique I elect to use. Touch is as important as technique.'

Then Srim Baba showed some fundamental forms. Obviously he had easy sledding demonstrating against frontal and rear bearhugs. Against a moving opponent – his student who appeared only for this portion of the activities – he would stroke with his left hand directly at the groin. Of course his opponent, standing above the blow, was forced to block it downwards with his left hand. Just as his block was fielding the initial blow, the right fist hit at the same point: too quickly and too near the blocking left hand for the right hand to stop it. Or both hands were launched at one time, sometimes downwards, or inwards, or outwards, but always focused on the groin. Sometimes a hand and foot were used in combination.

The student knew the system but was unable to stop these sequences. Baba could not be denied. No man in the world could have blocked him for long. The only

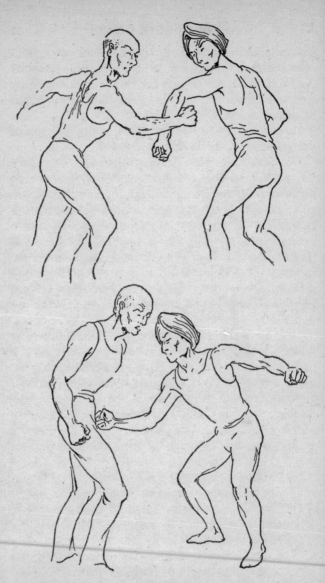

The Groin Strike – just a touch

chance would be to be good enough or lucky enough to blast him out of there before he got to your scrotum. And this would not be easy for he was fast, incredibly fast, and the punches you threw might be an *entrée* into his attack on the 'golden target'.

To indicate the prowess of Baba, let me tell you of the incident which closed our interview.

He said: 'Since this is the only time I shall ever show this method to anyone I should like to do something that you will remember. Something that will have impact on you.' (I thought: Here I am completely unnerved by what I have witnessed and he wants to give me something to remember him by!) 'Therefore I will promise that any trick you can do which involves the hands or arms, I can do also. This is the mark of a true master: not that he can do sleights that others cannot, perhaps because they have never tried, but that he can make his body do anything that someone else can do.'

This was a fine gesture, I thought. Unfortunately he was on rocky ground here. For it had long been a hobby of mine to learn any unusual and difficult gymnastic tricks that few others could perform. Through great exertions, I had become able to do possibly the hardest three gymnastic exercises in the world. Few people could do any one of them. So far as I knew I was the only one able to do *all* three. The exercises are:

(1) Extended push-up from prone position, fingertips and toes stretched as far as they will go.
(2) Five chin-ups on overhead bar using only one arm (I can use either arm).
(3) Rafter-walk for twenty-five feet. Using only fingers and thumbs, grasp overhead studding and supporting weight of body, go hand after hand for the required distance.

The reader is invited to try them. He will see that they are difficult because of the great stress put on the arms and hands.

I was tempted to go graciously without complying but I thought: he has issued the challenge. Let's see what he can do with it.

So, not attempting to disguise my pride, I showed the exercises.

When I was done he commented that it was a fair exercise. And then he did each one with an *élan* that I could not muster. There was no end to the man. With mixed emotions – crestfallen that he had achieved the tests and overawed by his ability to master his body – I bade farewell to him. I came away wiser.

5
STRANGLE OF
THE THUG

*'I will give you my opinion as to what I think necessary
to be done on such occasions,' said Sir Daniel Donnelly.
'First of all, you must take off your shirt' – Boxiana*

AFTER leaving the fistic palaces of Benares I journeyed
south to Hyderabad. I wanted to see Surbul Kormi,
who, rumour had it, had once been a flourishing Thug
– one who practised thuggee. I had researched thuggee
quite thoroughly years before and supposed that since
the British, under Colonel W. H. Sleeman, had
stamped it out by 1830, there could hardly be any
remnant extant.

But some things die hard. It turned out that Surbul
Kormi was very much a thuggee expert.

A Dutch professor of chemistry at Poona University,
J. Bluming (whose work on *cantharides* is without peer),
was able to introduce me to Kormi since Kormi's son
was a student of the good professor.

Kormi was an ugly man. I don't believe I have seen
a more ugly one. But his voice was soft and the fire in
his eyes diminished as he told me of thuggee one night
in 1952 at his residence. Bluming, acting as interpreter,
was the only other person present. Kormi talked in his
sad, soft voice. Following is the fruit of his talk.

'The origin of thuggee is disputed. However, I believe with the majority of my antecedents that the

Destructive Power in the world could not keep pace
with the Creative Power which peopled prolifically. So
the Destructive Power asked the Black Mother, the
Goddess Kali, for help. Kali demonstrated a strangle
with a cloth to her followers as the accepted mode of
dispatching victims. The idea here was to kill without
shedding blood since blood begets blood and creation
springs from it.

'We multiplied down through the years. Some of
our members became national heroes. Nizam-ud-din,
for example, saved Delhi from the Northern Invaders
in 1303 by his supernatural powers.

'My father was a Thug. When I was twelve he ini-
tiated me into the fraternity by having me swallow a
piece of coarse sugar we call gur. Gur is everything.
After taking it everyone's nature changes. I could do
anything I wished with my life after swallowing gur. I
could choose any profession – but I could not leave off
being a Thug. At the same time I swore fealty to Kali
and was presented with a *ruhmal* [yellow silken sash
about thirty-six inches long by one inch wide]. My
father adjured me that thuggee had been taboo through
his lifetime and would be so for all the future, therefore
I must keep this matter a stringent secret. Less than six
persons have learned of this in my lifetime and I am
now sixty-eight. What my son did in divulging it to
Professor Bluming was indiscreet in the extreme. But
that is past now.

'Once found out I thought the thing through and
decided that perhaps if I permitted Mr Gilbey an interview it would clarify thuggee for people in the West.
There are many misconceptions on it. For example, we
never drank blood and we never killed children and we
never killed wantonly. Though the result might be
death, the initial purpose was economic gain. All Kali

ever asked was that when we killed we use the strangle
rather than blood-letting weapons.

'Nowadays, Thugs are few. Probably there are less
than twelve in all India. Civilization is destroying us.
Who knows, in another generation thuggee may be
dead. My son will never be a Thug: I will not permit it.
Quite frankly, he does not have the talent for it.

'I called this an interview before. I have been guilty
of what Mr Churchill called a "terminological in-
exactitude". This is no interview. For I permit you no
questions or comments. Arbitrary, dogmatic, call it
what you will, I must have it this way. My stipulation
should not hurt you too much, however, since I hope
to anticipate most questions you would normally ask.

'For example, have I killed anyone? A poor
question, for by now you should know that thuggee is
not a theoretical exercise. It is practicality of the most
realistic sort. Of course I have killed people. Most of
this was when I was younger and needed the money.
Now I am comfortable enough to leave my *ruhmal* at
home. Civilization truly is stifling the art.

'Let me tell you of one case. It was only ten years
ago. I had met a young affluent barrister casually several
times. I did not like him. His breath was like a woman's.
He was rich and the women flocked around him: I did
not like him. So I plotted to remove him. I invited him
to my lodgings; not these, I was poorer then. He came
and we ate, drank and talked. When the drink appeared
to be telling on him, I edged ever closer. About this
time he left the room, weaving a bit, to heed the call of
nature. I awaited him – all the while plotting and
fingering the *ruhmal* in my pocket.

'Then the strangest thing happened. All of a sudden
I was pulled back strongly and the next moment *I* was
being strangled. There was no time for deliberation

The Terrible Kormi

and hardly time for escape. I tightened my neck muscles
which have always been strong from practising thuggee and threw myself to the side. This had the effect of
unbalancing my attacker and gave me distance and
leverage enough to get a foot into him. He released his
hold. I saw it was the barrister. Bringing my *ruhmal* out
of my pocket, I nabbed him on the first cast, went
behind him, and after a few spasmodic kicks he
expired. That *was* a coincidence and, reflecting on it
later, it frightened me. He was obviously a Thug with
the same intentions as mine. I was thankful that he was
young and therefore inexpert. For once an expert Thug
gets his *ruhmal* on your neck it is – as the Americans
say – curtains. There is no defence.'

At this juncture Kormi arose and walked to a bureau. Opening the top drawer he brought out two long pieces of silk. Returning, he handed them to us for examination.

'The one *ruhmal* is a standard one used for centuries by Thugs. The other is my modification of it. Notice how mine is the same except that it is notched or scalloped. This gives mine a better bite into a neck. And some necks are so muscular that you need every advantage you can get.

'Only once did I meet a neck which defied strangulation. The man must have been a wrestler or strong man type. Try as I might I could not choke him and all the time I was having trouble evading his huge hands. A man must be flexible. I picked up a stone and smashed at his skull with it. This dropped him and only then did strangulation suffice.'

Then Kormi demonstrated how he looped the *ruhmal* around a neck from in front, laterally, and from the rear. Needless to say the rear strangle was the best. But Kormi from any position was like lightning with the loop. It would take, I mused, a quick man to evade his noose. From the rear Kormi would hold the *ruhmal* in the middle with his left hand and make his silent approach.

Swinging his left hand from the right shoulder to the right side of his opponent's neck, he would catch the flying end of his sash with his right hand on the left side of his opponent's neck and thus effect a rear cross choke. If his victim were standing he would simultaneously put his knee into the small of his back and, jerking the head and shoulders back, break the spinal column. This is extremely drastic, however, and the reader is advised to leave it alone except when life itself is the issue.

Kormi ended his demonstration by saying I could use anything he had said but that I should disguise the name and locale unless he died before my work was issued. Because he died last October, I have been able to use factual particulars about this master of the deadly but dying art of thuggee.

6
THE MEXICAN KNIFE

'Genius is an infinite capacity for giving pains'
D. Herold

IF one were to make a partial list correlating national types and weapons, it would probably look like this:

> French – feet
> British – fists
> Koreans – head
> Americans – gun
> Irish – shilelagh
> Mexicans – knife

Such a list is subject to the defects of any generalization but I think few will quarrel with it.

The French came by their affinity for feet in the heyday of traditional French boxing (1825–1910); the British, their love of fists during the pugilistic period (1720–1900); and the American inclination for 'hardware' could probably be traced by an astute sociologist (of which I know none) to the use of same by police officers against recalcitrants. In order to compete, the latter armed and used. Later, the sub-sport of hunting made guns even more available. Today, any gawky youth who dislikes his dad's choice of TV channels can blast away.

No history gives the 'why' or 'when' for the others on the list. Presumably the Irish have always preferred a cudgel, and the Koreans, good headwork, in combat.

Certainly as far back as there is record the Mexican has tried conclusions with a knife in his hand. Indeed, the old story about the Negro who swiped at another with a razor* was old in Mexico before it was new in America. I don't know why the knife appeals to the Mexican any more than I know why the razor appeals to the Negro. I only know that it does – or did till it was prohibited by national ordinance in 1938.

And that is really the point of this chapter: what happens when the Mexican national weapon is proscribed? Some continue to use it, of course, to practise the old whirling forms and the short-fight tactics which made it lamentable for an American to enter the lists. Toby Rubin is the only one who lasted any time at all and that was only for six fights until that hot afternoon in Tijuana when he spilled his intestines. An American present, Al Miksos, told me later that the Mexican who did the job looked at Rubin lying there and said simply: 'The man has guts.' While his tense may have been wrong, his observation wasn't: Rubin's guts were much in evidence at that juncture.

But the practising and the fighting that was done was done surreptitiously, with an anxious eye ever out for the constabulary. A man could withdraw at any time with no loss of prestige and few of the fights ended in death. One I saw just missed though, both fighters in the end looking like they had been gored by a herd of fighting bulls. In a way it *was* honourable – much more

---

* I dislike dialect, so here it is in English. An esteemed Negro razor artist made a pass at an adversary. The latter laughingly said: 'Ha, you missed.' To which the artist replied: 'Yeah? Wait till you shake your head!'

so than bull killing* (I will not dignify that bestiality by calling it fighting) or cock matching (ditto). The antagonists were not coerced into it, they were not made angry as a preliminary, and, as I have said, they could bow out of further torture and subsequent death at any time.

However, I digress. Back to our muttons. After a time the prohibition had its impact. By 1948 the truly great knife fighters in Mexico could be numbered on the fingers of one hand.

José Gomez had been one of the great ones. After the art was outlawed José continued to practise but never again fought. The reason, he told me years afterwards, was that although he had been a good knifer he was an even greater Mexican. He chose to observe his country's laws.

But a fighter doesn't stop fighting. At the end of Tokugawa in Japan, when the *samurai* lost their swords, *kendo* and jujitsu really became popular. Many *samurai* simply changed weapons. And that is what José did. Oriented as he was to the knife, it was not surprising then that the weapon he chose, the out-stretched fingers of each hand, resembled his beloved knife.

This weapon, however, is not unique. The Indians, Chinese and Japanese, among others, possess it and put great value in it. But of all the fingertip methods I have seen, José's was superior on every count.

He knew anatomy, so he knew the targets on which

* This is not to say that many toreadors were not brave, fine men. Who can forget Juan Silveti, the 'Tiger of Guanajuato', who suffered thirty-two gorings during his career. Juan refused to discuss a lingering liver ailment with friends because, 'I don't want anyone to feel sorry for me. You feel sorry for animals, not men.' He died shortly afterwards.

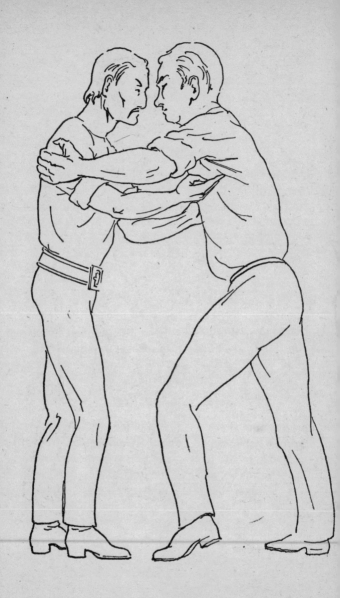

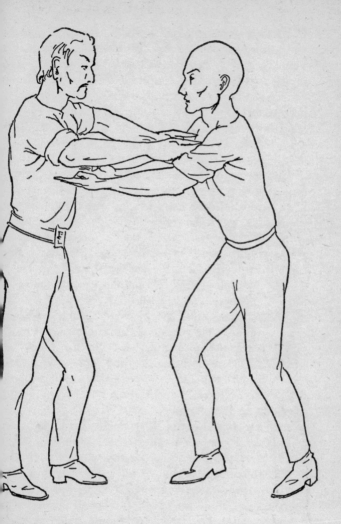

Two Knives in unison

to focus his attack. He knew posture and movement and was a dervish in defence. But above all he knew his weapon. He hardened those hands by exercising each finger to the utmost. He lifted prodigious weights progressively with each digit for hours every day. He performed thousands of push-ups on one finger of each hand at a time. He speared into a bucket of flour, then sand, and finally pebbles with his fingertips.

His weapon was the product of years. When he demonstrated for me he went through a piece of none-too-dry pine four inches thick and oak, one inch thick! With such solidity he had a terrible weapon. Its advantage is obvious. A fist shortens the attacking arc of the arm, fingertips extend it. A fist broadens the impact area and with more surface dissipates the shock. But extended fingertips concentrate the attack beautifully.

Moreover, fingertips do not stop at the surface. They dig, penetrate, probe – with disastrous effects for the inner organs. José did have peculiarities though. For example, when I pointed out that his knife must play havoc on the opponent's eyes he informed me that he never used his attack above the throat. Why? He told me that he made it a point that the opponent should see quite clearly who the victor was standing over him after each contest.

In this context I prefer to think that his knowledge of anatomy played a part in this grandiose reasoning. The head is nearly all bone and the eyes are relatively protected in bony sockets. Besides, the area from the pelvis to the chin offers many more lucrative targets and the knife does not have to travel so far, making defence against the opponent's counter more facile.

José stated that his system was all his own. He had borrowed from no one. Then he made a slight amendment. From an unidentified Chinese source he obtained medicine which he took daily and religiously. The hardening of the fingertips, he told me – and I had heard the same from countless Chinese – often brought on blindness. So he had thought it prudent to make this one concession, but only after his eyes had nearly failed early in the training regimen.

Here is one method José showed me. When your opponent comes in close (especially in a frontal bear-hug) bring the right spear up into his left side and, simultaneously, spear either under his right arm or the side of his throat with your left fingertips. The right palm is held up; the left one, down. These knives are brought inwards with power emanating from the shoulders. This trick can really tear a man up, believe me.

The reader may ask whether it is better to knife with palm up or down. José said that it mattered very little, though he favoured the palm down method when attacking the throat.

This is all I got from a man inclined to be secretive and laconic but who paid a debt by talking and demonstrating. Today he is on the wrong side of sixty, still living in the torrid heat of that small town (he asked me not to disclose its name), and probably still fighting when the occasion demands. The last I heard he had had fourteen victorious fights and the figure now is probably double that. An old man certainly, but with those magnificent weapons he will go to his grave much older still.

7
PARISIAN HALITOTIC ATTACK

'Lives there a man with breath so dread . . .' – A. Smith

EVERY chapter in this book represents my experience and doing save for the present one. It happened to Donn Draeger, a truthful man certainly, and a man known across the globe for his research in the fighting arts. What follows is culled from a letter Donn wrote me in 1953.

. . . Jacques later introduced me to Henri Pougard – a most ordinary looking man with a most unusual speciality. He lived in a small walk-up apartment on Saint Marguerite Street and was a draughtsman by trade. He was a graded judo man and full of ideas on the subject of self defence. Henri and I spent many pleasant evenings together.

Then one evening while we were sipping absinthe in his flat, I asked him the innocuous question which set his eyes to sparkling: how important was specialized breathing to efficient fighting? He responded to the effect that over-stress on the breathing aspect might deter development of the entire art. And then he said, 'But I have a secret art in which breathing is nearly *all*.'

I sipped my drink slowly. I had learned the lesson you taught me well, John – that of never appearing anxious. 'Oh,' I said, 'what do you mean?'

He leaned over and brought his head closer to mine. There was a sharpness about his breath that could not have come from absinthe. But I paid that no heed. I listened.

'You will agree that the most subtle form of defeat is that which comes through suggestion, chiefly through an hypnotist. The contact here is long range and effected through the eyes of the operator. Or sometimes his voice. I think you will agree that this is possible.

'If so, you can hardly cavil with the idea that a man may be defeated perhaps even more easily by a shout (as in Japanese *kiai-jutsu*) which has proportionally greater force and contact than hypnotism. We know that a soprano who achieves notes of a very high register can shatter a plate-glass window. Thus only a fool would quarrel with the belief that a gifted man can injure another human with a properly attuned shout.

'Taking this process a bit further, I created an art which narrowed the focus by increasing the contact, but which still fell short of actual physical touch. Simply stated, my art is to cultivate an evil breath which under certain circumstances (for example, it will not work in a windstorm) I can direct at a human with drastic results.

'I had first to create the breath. This took two years of experimenting with various foods and herbs. During this time I tested my weapon against stray dogs and cats. Only when I was able to make them faint from ten feet *in the open air* did I feel competent to tackle humans. At first it was more difficult than with animals but I persisted three more years and finally triumphed.

'You cannot know much of olfaction so let me be

Henri Pougard, master of the incredible

technical for just a moment. Smell stimuli go directly
to the sensory receptor cells located in the olfactory
epithelium of the upper nasal cavity, but they must dis-
solve in the mucus which overlies the receptor cells in
order to activate the cells. This activation is merely
accentuated by the varieties – sweet, sour and sharp –
of smell and does not affect the senses sufficiently to
cause unconsciousness. The mechanism which pro-
duces that is actually a reflexive action which brings on
respiratory inhibition. The reflex is the result of

stimulation of trigeminal nerve endings by selected odours. This is what causes fainting.

'I had many problems. I got so I could produce nausea indoors, then dizziness, and finally fainting. But outdoors it was much more difficult. When I finally got across this hurdle, I still faced my biggest problem. At first, I could not use the weapon except within four hours of ingesting my special diet. You can see the pitfalls in this. If danger threatened I could not very well ask my antagonist to desist while I ate, could I?

'So I began to break the formula down and to eat a little at each meal. After a great deal of experimentation, I succeeded. I am now able to bring my evil breath into play by abdominal pressure whenever it is needed.

'I tell you I like it. As a method of self defence it is effective, sure, and practically painless. If I will it, my victims will awaken unhurt.'

To shorten the story, John, I then asked Henri for a demonstration of this power. He consented. He opened the three windows wide, and snapped on an electric fan which fronted us from a dresser.

Then he got a studied expression on his face and seemed to concentrate for perhaps thirty seconds. Then, from across his dining room table – a distance of about six feet – he breathed on me.

I watched him, my senses acute. I thought, what a big mouth when opened wide; almost like Joe E. Brown. Then the odour, smell, no – stink – hit me. A garbage dump, rendering plant, tannery – this beat them all. Of course I didn't have time to analyse it then. For the onslaught of that stink was like a physical strike. I gasped for breath that wasn't there, gasped again with the same result, and fainted.

I woke to Henri's laughing banter and, feeling foolish, took the glass of absinthe he proffered me. I acknowledged that he had 'killed' me and adjured him not to gloat since I felt like I had been caught in the Easter Parade without even a fig leaf! We proceeded to taste the nectar of high inebriation! I really needed it. I wanted to forget.

As I want to forget even now. For, believe this, John, when I recall that moment I am so revulsed that I begin to feel giddy. If I dwelled on it I know I would cop out again. So I run from it, and fast. To me this 'killing by remembering' is even more astonishing than the attack itself.

I am somewhat nauseous now from writing about it. But there should be a record made. I knew you would want to know. But one favour, John, please. Tell anyone you like about this, but don't ever mention it to me. Please. I want to forget.

8
THE CANTON CORKSCREW

'Into the midst of things' – Horace

ANY *karate* master worth his salt will acknowledge the
efficiency of the seemingly effortless 'soft' whiplash
punches of various Chinese boxers they have met. The
speed of these punches belies their power. In reality
they are not as soft as they appear. Most of these boxers
practise one form or another of ancient *shaolin*. *Karate*
itself is but one small form of this varied and multi-
formed system. In older *shaolin* the fist was actually only
a small part, say one-tenth, of the whole, greater
priority being placed on the open hand and other components.

Despite this, the fist part of *shaolin* is economical and
efficient. The fist is hardened and 'formed' and then
meshed into countless leading, countering and combination sequences. I have spent hundreds of hours in
learning these moves and must accord them a high
place in the realm of unarmed combatives.

But the ear is an enemy. In a discussion of *shaolin*
fistics one autumn day in Manila in 1954, an old
Chinese present, bald and nearly gone in the eyes, mentioned *hsing-i*. I queried him on this method. He knew
little, he said, but he knew a merchant on the east side,
Wong Mu-ta, reputedly the leading master of this form

in the Philippines. Could he arrange an interview? He
kindly agreed.

Wong Mu-ta had a small textiles establishment,
clean but not neat. The man himself was the same.
About 240 pounds of obesity, his hair set on a fleshy
face looked like it had been combed with a towel. And
his garb was clean but in some disarray as it tried but
failed to encompass the proportions of the man. At
first glance I nearly surrendered any chance of success
in the interview.

His manner, however, was better than his appearance. Very genial, he seated us and had brandy in our
hands before our buttocks relaxed in the cushions. So
I wanted to learn *hsing-i*! He would be my happy
mentor and, he added with ostentatious satisfaction, at
no charge.

I hastened to interject that I had to leave Manila in
less than a month. So I couldn't hope to learn even the
principles in such a short period. What I wanted was a
demonstration of this system and possibly a compari-
son of it with *shaolin*.

Wong snorted at this even though his friend seated
beside me was a noted *shaolin* boxer.

'*Shaolin*,' he said, 'originally was a fine system but it
has now degenerated into strictly a strong arm external
business, whereas *hsing-i* is an internal method, softer,
more subtle, and much more efficient. *Shaolin* depends
on external strength, power, and impetus. *Hsing-i* does
not. With *hsing-i* you have no need for leverage. You
can punch the opponent from inches away with
greater effect than a *shaolin* boxer can from a foot
away.'

I broke in. 'What you say is in defiance of all
Western boxing concepts. We have short punches, but
it is simply impossible to generate enough power to

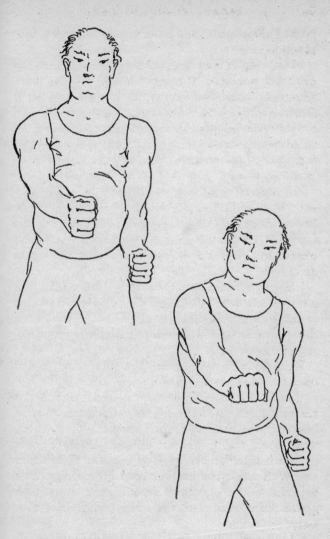

The Canton Corkscrew

hurt an opponent from a few inches away. I find this hard to believe.'

He smiled. 'The answer of course lies in demonstration. But first let me verbalize it. In Western boxing and in *shaolin* you punch straight away, essentially on a line. But in *hsing-i* we punch differently. We punch against the internal organs, not against the external framework. Thus our punches have more focus and more effect. If we punch with unreserved power we cannot guide or focus our punch. Therefore, using our body in perfect concert with the punch aligned to our opponent's posture, we attack his vital organs. But words never accomplish the job. Let me show you.'

So saying, Wong Mu-ta demonstrated the varied techniques of *hsing-i*. It was brisk and delightful. For me, the most remarkable was the corkscrew fist punch. It was a variant of basic *hsing-i* learned by Wong in Canton years before. I describe it for the reader.

Double both fists in the orthodox manner but keep the knuckles aligned vertically rather than horizontally. Spread your legs so that your feet are within the line of your shoulders. Extend your right arm almost to its full length but still bent at the elbow, the right fist on a line with your nose but somewhat lower. Now you should be within three inches of your opponent's midriff.

With no appreciable thought of strength, focus the strike on his navel and extend your arm, simultaneously screwing your fist a quarter turn counterclockwise (to the left). Be sure that the screw is kept to a quarter turn since any more could well have fatal consequences. This screwing focuses the punch internally, and directs it at the small intestine and, more deeply, the pancreas. The screwing has to mesh smoothly with the extension of the arm.

This will not be learned in a day, a week, or a month. But if the reader can practise it an hour a day he can master it. One necessary ingredient – the generation and utilization of *ch'i* – will be discussed in the next section since it is too complex a subject to be brought in here.

But, believe me, the Orientals don't have a corner on this art. I now have the ability to screw with either hand. Others also. In Tokyo in 1961 a Professor of English, William Fuller, sought me out and asked me if I knew *hsing-i*. When I responded that I knew a little he volunteered the fact that he had studied the cork-screw for over a decade. Then he asked if I would 'feel' his technique. I agreed.

He went into the basic stance and caressed me with his right fist. The effect was instantaneous. I bent over and retched. I had not eaten for several hours, other-wise I would have tossed it all then and there. The corkscrew punch, short and sweet. The highest form of the boxing art. Learn it, cultivate it, but beware of its dangers!

9
A METHOD OF INCREASING CH'I

'In motion, be like water
At rest, like a mirror
Respond, like the echo
Be subtle, as though non-existent'
Taoist verse

CH'I, or intrinsic energy, underlies most Asian martial arts. It is the very basis of *t'ai ch'i* and *aikido* and permeates many other systems. In China the so-called internal boxing schools make the most use of it but even *shaolin* sects espouse it.

In travelling around I found that every system had a different approach to the concept of *ch'i*, some slight but others great. And so as I looked I tried to find a common principle, a method that I could pass on. I believe I found it and I happily give it to the reader.

I don't propose to write a philosophic treatise on *ch'i* here. Space does not permit it, nor inclination urge. Suffice to say that *ch'i* is inner, intrinsic energy, which brings pliability not rigidity with it. I can still remember the repetitious admonitions, 'No power! No power!' of a Chinese boxing master of the White Crane system. And yet his arms which whipped me from pillar to post and seemed power-filled, were not. Indeed, the Chinese say that the utilization of *ch'i* should bring one the pliability of an infant.

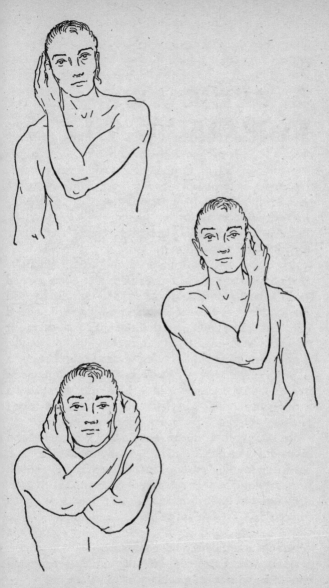

Creating Ch'i

Ch'i when accumulated in the *tan t'ien* (a point just below the navel) and used properly has the quality of massed wind or water. This is achieved through mass integration. The effect can be enormous. I have seen *ch'i* do amazing things but, since these fall outside our scope, I leave them unsaid.

The best and quickest way to lay in a store of *ch'i* is simply the following exercise which I derived from Indo-Chinese sources. Choose a quiet room where you will not be disturbed. Turn down the lights and for fifteen minutes a day (it must be every day!) perform the following exercise.

Sit down comfortably. Relax your body and time your inhalation/exhalation cycles so that they do not exceed ten a minute. Breathe in through the nose and out through the mouth, but inaudibly. Your tongue should adhere to the roof of your mouth. Now take your left hand and cover your right ear well but not tightly. Breathe slowly and think of only one thing – *relaxation*. After five minutes reverse your hand and ear: your right hand now covers your left ear. Breathe and concentrate loosely as before. After five minutes cross your arms, covering both ears, your right arm on the outside of your left, and do this for five minutes.

And that is all. Too simple, you say? Believe me, if you have a choice in life and, especially in self defence, choose the simple method. True, this exercise lasts but fifteen minutes and involves no contortionist yogic acrobatics, but this can be said for it: it works! Within fourteen days (just two weeks!) you will notice:

(1) Your tongue becomes semi-rigid.
(2) Your palm(s) in contact with your ear(s) become cool; when not in contact, they will sweat.

(3) Your entire body will become light and airy and
    you will feel that you can levitate.

The things you will not notice will be even more
significant. Your arms will fill with *ch'i*, your body will
become pliable, and your movement will be expedited
greatly. But these things will take longer.

I remind you. This must be done every day. And you
must relax, slump, droop. Otherwise progress will not
come. But if you practise it faithfully, your body will
become healthier and more powerful and your self-
defensive skill will increase appreciably.

10
THE MACEDONIAN BUTTOCK

'Thy impudence hath a monstrous beauty, like the hindquarters of an elephant' – *J. E. Flecker*

SOME there are who contend that it is far better to learn one method of self defence thoroughly than it is to learn a little about several methods. They argue that a common current runs through all systems and that the same basic principles underlie all methods irrespective of national origin. I will not argue with this. It is true that the same principles govern but there *are* differences in application and the French say a mouthful when they say, '*Vive la différence!*' These ramifications are what led me to search out the grand masters of these varied fighting forms throughout the world.

In searching them out I found, unsurprisingly, that almost every method contains some unfunctional bilge. In the reader's own search he must be careful to separate the useful from the merely attractive. Generally, if a technique requires a great deal of space or several distinct moves, mark it down as unfunctional. Many can do what others cannot, but often what they do is useless. The following story from Plutarch will illustrate my meaning.

A traveller at Sparta, standing upon one leg, said to

a Lacedaemonian, 'I do not believe you can do as much.'

'True,' said he, 'but every goose can.'

And while we are in Greece let me tell you of a man with an amazing technique. George Kostandis is a medium-level official in the Greek government. In the basement of his ample home in Salonika he has a fairly complete physical culture gym with weights, mats, and other paraphernalia. In college he had been both national boxing and national wrestling champion.

I spent two days with this short, burly bit of brawn in 1948, sampling the self defence method he taught to a few selected pupils. The system was for the most part routine, drawn largely from European and American sources. Normally it would not have held me more than a couple of hours. I remained two days because (a) George was such a perfect host, and (b) of a unique method employing waist and buttock he taught. Since this book is not a travelogue, we can skip a delineation of the delights under (a) – pausing only to say that Greek women *are* underrated – and move to (b).

The Kostandis method was based on a very simple principle: power dissipates the further it has to travel from its source. Body power is transmitted chiefly from the waist region and, when relayed through the hands or feet, loses most of its initial strength. Why not utilize the region near the waist if it is more powerful? Such answers that you put yourself too close to the opponent's counter or that the waist region cannot be hardened are not satisfactory since (1) if you are very close, the opponent does not have the leverage to effectively counter, and, (2) the buttocks can be hardened admirably for use in striking.

The student is first taught how to harden his but-

Kostandis's Famed Buttock

tocks. In standing and in walking he holds a coin between the parts which are pinched inward. This trick
learned, he spends an hour a day banging his butt
against a huge sandbag. He uses both sides, sliding
either forwards obliquely or directly or from the side.
Energy is concentrated and expended by synchronizing
the slide with the projecting of the hip and buttock.
The force generated is immense and I saw many
students actually thrown into the air by the swift un-
dulation of an attacker's buttock.

In applying force the student is taught to project
through the target, as if he were trying to hit something
directly behind the opponent. This idea is common to
Asian striking methods and I would say it is quite
valid.

Next, approach and target(s). The technique can be
used after countering a strike when you close with your
opponent either directly or obliquely from the front.
Invariably most street fights will at some point find the
antagonists locked in close. The buttock is the natural
weapon here. It requires little space for 'windup' and
can be delivered as a surprise since the opponent will
be watching your hands or feet.

The buttock can be used as a displacer – a movement
which knocks the opponent off balance and opens him
to the next attack in your sequence – or as a finisher. As
a finisher you aim at the opponent's groin or his lower
abdomen. In this case you must control the opponent
by pulling him towards you with your arms at the same
time you attack.

The buttock attack can be a vicious thing with terrible results. Any doctor will tell you that it takes considerable force to break a pelvis. Yet Kostandis told
me that three of his pupils had broken attackers' pel-
vises with this technique. One victim – all were hooli-

gans bent on robbery at night – almost died since both his bladder and urethra were ruptured to boot.

The attack can be made from the side as well as from the front. Usually this approach will mean that the attack is a displacer rather than a finisher, since the opponent's leg impedes delivery to the vital groin area.

Kostandis is no braggart. I believed his narration totally. Especially when he punctuated it with demonstrations involving those powerful buttocks. He told me that a local giant in a nearby town some years before had taken to calling at all the taverns and night-clubs challenging any and all to combat. This was bad enough, but the brazen one wasn't content with a room full of silence and would yank some innocent from his chair and punish him severely in front of the rest. His strength was such that when the police early on sought to curb him, they sent four of their beef trust against him. The giant put two in the hospital and the other two were not of any use to either the police force or their wives for three months! After that the police gave him a wide berth.

His town conquered, the giant invaded Salonika. And so it happened that one night he barged into a tavern where Kostandis and his fiancée (this was many years before: when I was there the pair had four children) were seated having an after-the-theatre drink. The giant propelled his 260 pounds front and centre and announced his usual challenge. Kostandis's fiancée, sensing trouble, murmured that it would be better if they left and he, a wise man, concurred.

The pair got up from their table and started to move off when, unluckily, the behemoth saw them.

'You,' he said, pointing a finger as big as a hand at Kostandis, 'I'm going to whip you.'

Kostandis pushed the girl away from him and said

with great panache: 'Don't let anything but fear stop you.'

The giant had never been spoken to that way before. He grabbed Kostandis and threw him into the wall. Then – but let Kostandis tell it.

'I rebounded nicely from this exhilarating twirl and then the oaf made his big mistake. He could have stood off and pulverized me with those huge fists and perhaps been successful but no, his pride had been hurt, and he couldn't spare the time for a neat job. So foolishly he closed with me, grabbed me again, and yanked me close. I didn't even have to pull him. I merely rode his pull in and applied the buttock flush on his pubes. He looked at me unbelievingly, released his grip, and went forwards like an Olympic diver. They carried him out on a stretcher and he spent weeks in a hospital. I would like to say that this comeuppance changed his character, but it didn't. Six months later the man was imprisoned for life for armed robbery.'

The story bears out the efficiency of the technique taught by Kostandis. It is close combat of the highest order. Yet let me warn you again of its deadliness. In practising be careful when working 'live'. Use your power on the sandbag.

11
THE MVD
SPECIAL

'Excellence is the perfect excuse' – R. W. Emerson

N. SLYMANSKI came over to the West on a beautiful defection coup during the Hungarian Revolution in 1956. I should say after the Revolution, for Slymanski stood shoulder to shoulder with the Freedom Fighters until Budapest fell to the combined weight of Russian tanks.

Slymanski was quite an acquisition. He had spent years in the Soviet security services and knew the inner workings of that apparatus as well as any man alive. So Washington plumbed, probed, processed. And after they were through the Russian went to a small Iowa college to teach the thing he knew best – wrestling.

For Slymanski was the best wrestler Russia has turned out in the last decade. His position in the MVD prevented him competing internationally but he kept up daily practice. They still talk about the afternoon he dumped Mazur, Bogdan and four other prominent heavyweights one after the other. These were the best in the world and he went through them without effort. He was so good that he refused to accept a win by decision points. If he didn't pin you he felt he hadn't truly triumphed. The pin signified victory. The few men who survived the first meeting were always pinned decisively on a later occasion. He was such a rage in Russia that limousines with mayors waited for him.

I had an afternoon with Slymanski in that small Iowa college town in 1957. An erect six-footer, he still weighed an even 200 pounds. We had food and vodka (just because you forsake communism doesn't mean you relinquish the better things of Russian life) brought in. His English was passable and my Russian – my renditions of excerpts from Pushkin and Lermontov delighted him – filled in the gaps.

We talked the wrestling thing into the ground and then he launched into a dissertation on *sambo*, the Russian form of judo. This jacket wrestling, patterned on traditional Russian wrestling and Japanese jujitsu, will compete in the 1964 Tokyo Olympics with orthodox Japanese judo and, from what Slymanski said about it, I hesitate to prophesy which form will prevail.

When we had wearied this point I asked him about the Russian 'minor sport' of face slapping. I had heard that in 1931 in Kiev two friends in a vodka joint began playfully slapping one another alternately. The force and frequency increased but neither man would call it quits. The slapping continued. Finally, thirty hours and three referees later the then referee announced, 'This is silly, go home.' And they did.

Slymanski laughed. It was true, he said, face slapping contests still are held. The incident I had mentioned, between Bexbordky and Goniusz, in 1931, was still the record time. It had lasted so long because neither man knew the proper way to slap. I tended to agree since I had once seen a raw-necked buck private slap a husky California street-fighter into unconsciousness with one blow back in 1941.

Then Slymanski told me of a man named Sobotka, a

Sambo, *the Russian version of judo*

master of the quick kill, who trained MVD apprentices
in the devious dodges of destruction.

'There was an American film years ago, *Beau Geste*.
Did you see it?' he asked.

I said I had.

'Well you probably remember the scar-faced Ser-
geant Markov who made life in the French Foreign
Legion a hell for all the recruits. He was a tough task-
master and at one juncture someone remarked that he
had been kicked out of the MVD for cruelty.'

I remembered the line. Brian Donlevy had played
the part well. I laughed.

But he enjoined me not to laugh. Sobotka, he said,
had been the living counterpart of the fictional Markov.
He had been kicked out of the Russian secret service
not once, but twice, for 'over-zealousness'. Some-
how, however, he kept coming back.

It was Sobotka who had shown him the way to slap
a man once and bring him to his knees. As Slymanski
described it, the trick here is to slap with a cupped open
hand. If you slap with stretched fingers you cover more
surface but you lose concentration and, more important, you lose the power transmitted through the
cupped enclosure. Force is accentuated by bringing
your power from the turn of the waist rather than from
the arm alone.

When you slap, the air is compacted by the force
exerted and the power effect is multiplied. It is important to keep the thumb closely glued to the index
finger. The facial nerves of even an experienced boxer
cannot withstand this effect.

I mentioned that this was the kind of blow that Fair-
bairn and others in the West were teaching during
World War II. But they directed the blow at the
opponent's ears because of the vacuum it created and

the terrible damage it caused the inner ear. The ideal of
course was to creep silently up behind a sentry and,
cupping both hands, slap both of his ears simultaneously.

The Russians taught the same method, he said. The
face slap is simply an amplification. The only difference
is the target, since the cupping itself induces the
vacuum which energizes the effect. So you get a
vacuum either way, but in the one method the inner
ear is attacked; in the other, your aim is to act upon the
facial nerves.

Technically, he pointed out, the pain induced is intense. The force penetrates deep inside the head to a
central knot of facial nerves called the 'gasserian
ganglion'. This knot is headquarters for the nerves of
sensation that serve the eye, the upper jaw, and the
lower jaw. When the knot is disturbed by a blow it
causes real havoc: you can't focus your eyes, your
orientation sense goes awry, and often you lose con-
sciousness. This last is something of a blessing for the
pain that ensues is the same maddening, merciless pain
of *tic douloureux* (facial neuralgia), called by many
doctors the worst pain a human can experience.

Sobotka told him that there had been men he could
not knock down with his fists but there had never been
a man he couldn't up-end with the slap. Slymanski said
that this worthy never minced words. He believed him.
And from what I had heard of him and knew of Slymanski, I do too.

12
THE UNEXPECTED TACTIC

'Employing every tooth and claw
In the awfullest way you ever saw . . .'
E. Field

'TRUE,' the dirty man observed, 'self defence is having a vogue – a real damned fad. *Karate*, *savate*, and all these other methods are really pulling them in. I have nothing against 'em either. They're cracking good systems.'

We were sitting in a bar in Johannesburg in the spring of 1954. The man across from me was in his forties, slight but wiry – and again let me say – dirty. From his forehead down to his thickly encrusted fingernails he was as grimy as a miner. Strangely, that was his name – Josh Miner. He was a fairly wealthy land-owner and had no right to be dirty. But every time I saw him he was.

I point this out to the reader merely to show him that he must take his experts as they come. If you want to borrow their virtues you can hardly be affronted by their vices. There is no common mould for fighters.

Dr W. Backhus of Miami had given me *entrée* to Josh Miner. Backhus had said, 'Go see him. You'll find a man. A successful one too. He's been in countless street fights, still responds to every challenge, and to date he hasn't even been tied!'

So here we were together at last. And Josh Miner, the invincible fighter, was talking.

'These methods I say are OK. But you know what they lack? Surprise, that's what. Oh, they're diverse enough I guess, but I've practised most of them and I say that the sequences are predictable. And that isn't good, friend. Do you know why I've never been beaten?'

Before I could offer a polite negative, he took a breath and went on.

'I've never been beaten because I've always fought a fight my opponent didn't know. I mean I do the un-expected and it gets 'em every time. Take for example judo. Now I know you're highly graded in judo and probably worth it, but, believe me, it has its limita-tions. I've come afoul of several black belts in street combat and they're sitting ducks.'

'That easy, eh?' I broke in, a bit peeved at his con-fident air.

'Right-o,' he said, a smile cutting a swathe across that dirty face. 'But already I can see your disbelief. I'm no theoretician. I can demonstrate. Now, later – you name it.'

Here his smiling eyes grew hard. But it was a chal-lenge and I responded with a stony stare. I thought of Finley Peter Dunne's classic statement: 'You can refuse to love a man or to lend him money, but if he wants to fight you have got to oblige him.' Attuning my voice to my stare I said, 'Let's hear you out. We can fight later.'

As though he had never been interrupted, he re-sumed his story.

'I was saying that judo has definite limitations in the street. I cite a few. Chap in Pretoria, three-dan I hear, called me a couple years back. We squared off. I ap-

proached him with my left hand going for his right
sleeve and my right for his left lapel, my hands open
and arms relaxed, understand. Orthodox judo I believe. But this was the street, not a judo mat! You
know what that fool did? He followed my lead auto-
matically, extending his arms and hands to take hold.
Komi – how do you say?'

'*Kumi-kata*,' I said.

'Right. Well, to shorten the story, he never got hold.
I belted him out, my right chopping his kidney and my
left hooking to his carotid artery. Short and significant, eh?'

I couldn't suppress a smile. 'Quite so. How about
the other judo gents?'

He ordered another round, passed a calloused hand
across his perspiring brow, and responded.

'They also slept – before and after. Habit is an in-
sidious thing. It reduces a man's flexibility and in the
street that's bad. How'd I beat them? The same way –
surprise. The first bird, we locked on and I spun in for
the inner thigh throw, whatever you call it in Japan,
and he merely braced, confident of sweeping my feet as
I retracted from the unsuccessful throw. But, poor
fool, I wasn't throwing: I was kicking! After my pivot
I whacked up with my right foot, catching him flush in
his privates and he died for several minutes.'

He took a helluva slug of his stout and I did the same.

'Go on,' I urged him. 'I find this stimulating.'

'Right,' he said, his eyes narrowing, 'and I hope you
also find it believable. No matter. I'll prove my system
to you when we come to conclusions later. The other
judo player I served the same way, only with that
stomach throw; you know, where you take hold and
then sit down, putting your foot on his stomach and
rolling backwards?'

Josh Miner

'*Tomoenage*,' I said, 'only for better leverage the foot should be placed lower than the stomach.'

'It was,' he rejoined, broadly smiling, 'it was. Much lower. Now this proves the value of my surprise thesis. If I had straightway tried to kick him he would have dodged. But we locked on in the judo manner and I began the stomach throw and all he did was brace slightly to resist a throw that wasn't a throw. I sat down on my heel and thrust my foot squarely into his genitalia. That ended it, of course.'

I nodded and remarked: 'Chinese boxers say you can't put *ch'i* there and without *ch'i* you're nothing.'

We finished our drinks and then he drove me to the outskirts of the sprawling city to a rundown farmstead where one of his hired hands lived. On the way I chided him for telling me so much about his method. He only observed in answer: 'Surprise has no limitations.'

I outweighed him by at least eighty pounds. But even with that advantage and with years of learning varied and vicious ways of fighting behind me I was a bit worried. I liked to fight. But I want a man to fight in a logical, albeit ruthless, manner. This damned surprise thesis was unsettling.

After signing a typed waiver (Miner, with all his street fights, could have saved money by having them mimeographed) and agreeing to discontinue only when one of us was unconscious – we squared off.

Now this book is not meant as self-advertisement. It isn't even autobiographical, except incidentally. So I draw a veil on much of the combat which followed. And really there wasn't much. It was a short fight. I knew, or at least felt fairly sure that Miner would not lead. I also knew that he would be pretty set for *karate* or Chinese techniques. Whatever I used had to be sure: with Miner there would be no second chance. He despised and had been successful against judo. So I decided to surprise him by using judo. But after locking on, to attack before he did.

Add to this the fact that I knew I couldn't fool him long. He knew judo. And his reflexes were probably razor-sharp. So, to be doubly sure, I planned to feint with one throw and, accepting his defensive push, turn it into a throw in the direction of his push. Judo men will recognize this principle in the combination of *ouchi-seoinage*. Another surprise for this master of the unexpected!

We circled guardedly and locked on. 'Judo, is it?' he snarled, but by then I was going forwards with *ouchi. Ouchi* is simply a throw hooking your opponent's left leg with your right from inside and driving him directly back. I placed the hook well and drove in to the pile of concrete that was Miner. But this figure is false, for the concrete moved. It moved exactly where I wanted it – directly forwards. I pivoted, went low, and Miner went over the top. At his zenith, I released my hands, and he crashed into the dirt on his shoulder and neck.

Miner lay where he fell. He was hurt and a funny sound came from his lips. I rolled him over, saw he was conscious, and prepared to choke him out. After all, that had been the agreement – the fight not to end till one of us was unconscious. Warily I rolled him over but I had no need to fear: he was really far gone. Shock had glazed his eyes and his right shoulder hung crazily. Kneeling there, I started to insert for a lapel choke and he opened his eyes and spoke.

'No need,' he gasped. 'I've been there.'

I inserted. 'The agreement was that one should be unconscious.'

'Wait, wait,' he said, 'damn the agreement. Man, do I look like a viable fighter?' Here the strangest thing happened. Josh Miner began to cry. Big rivulets of tears exploded from his eyes.

Nonplussed a bit, I relaxed and drew back. What a spectacle, I thought, the invincible weeping like a woman! But that is all I thought. From another life, another existence, came the unexpected. The 'incapacitated' Miner merely lay there and kicked me squarely in the groin. I passed out instantly. I had been kicked and hit there before but never so beautifully and had never passed out.

Ten minutes later I was able to crawl awhile, then stand; stand awhile, then walk. And I went away from there. But not until I found that tersely worded note from Miner. Terse, hell. There was just one word written on a blank square of notepaper. The word: SURPRISE!

13
THE CHAVANTE ARMLOCK

'The effective use of violence implies a preponderance of destructive power at vital places through the entire operation' – H. Lasswell

THAT year I had time for a trip to South America but not time enough to visit both the Jivaro Indians of Peru and the Chavantes of Brazil. I tossed a coin and the Chavantes had me for better or worse.

Sao Paulo on the Tiete River was like any other city of two million souls – big and crowded and noisy. I stayed only long enough to get the forms and introductory letters necessary to visit the Chavantes in their element.

A week later I was in the Amazonian rain forest, a guest of a large colony of semi-nude Chavantes and one bored Brazilian Interior Ministry functionary who acted as my interpreter.

The Chavantes are little known and little studied. They wear breech-clouts (in that heat it could be argued that even these are too much!), live in thatched huts, and use bow and spear to hunt. The *Encyclopedia Britannica*, which I dearly love, calls them 'rather timid hunting folk'.

You can't be right too often. The Chavantes are *not* timid. True, they don't war on neighbouring tribes but this is because they don't have to: (1) their neighbours, who live in mortal dread of them, steer clear of Chavante land, and (2) the Chavantes work off their 'aggressions' (as a six-cocktail-a-day Chicago psychiatrist would say) through their unique form of wrestling/fighting called *panmo*.

Panmo was what I had come to see and I got my fill. It is a standing form of wrestling/fighting done without garb of any kind. Ground wrestling is not permitted but that is about its only prohibition other than that eye-gouging and striking the groin are also vetoed. There is no delineated ring area by which you can gain points by pushing your opponent out, as in *sumo*. *Panmo* insists on throwing or striking your opponent so that he is forced to the ground. It is the ancient *pankratium* in all its unrestricted fury. Injuries are frequent but, surprisingly, fatalities are not. But men, good men, *have* died doing it.

Every tribe member wrestles. They always have and presumably always will. A non-playing spectator is unheard of. Even the cripples practise those parts of the art within their physical capabilities. Women, however, do not wrestle and there is a heavy taboo against their even witnessing matches.

As I said, I came and saw. And was thrilled. Though violent, the *panmo* experts were truly skilled. They knew how to grapple; their throws were graceful and their striking methods effective. Their kicking did not approach that of a *capoeiragem* expert – but whose does? It wasn't too long before I noticed a singular thing. Many of the wrestlers were having their arms broken by an *atemi*-like armlock which was effected by their opponents' two hands. It was quick and it was powerful.

The chief of the tribe, who had been acting as my guide, noticed my interest.

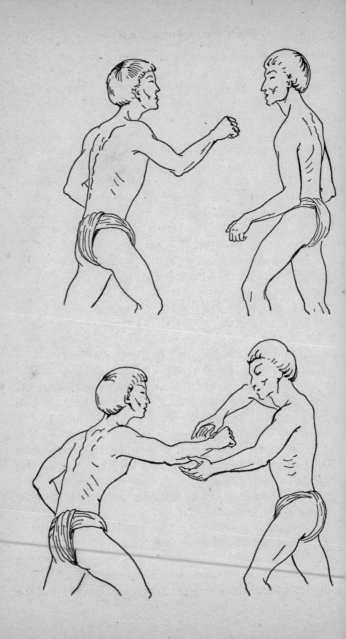

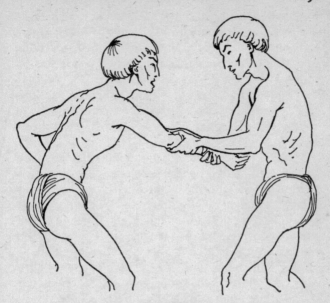

Short and sweet – the Chavante Armlock

'You have seen the effects of the Chavante armlock.
Would you say it is as effective as other methods you
have seen?'

I said it certainly was.

Then the chief asked whether I had seen Rargentine
Arocca wrestle. I said no but I had seen him *act*. He
laughed loud and long.

Then he asked: 'What does Arocca use mainly when
he acts?'

I rejoined that he used his feet chiefly.

'Do you know why he uses his feet?'

'No,' I said, 'I suppose it's more sensational or it
lends a certain uniqueness to his performance.'

He said that this was partially true no doubt but the

main reason was because both of his arms were maimed as a result of a match with a Chavante in 1948! Arocca had thought to make mincemeat of the slender, smooth-muscled Indian and in forty seconds was on his back with both arms broken.

'To prove this,' he said with eyes shining, 'the next time you see Arocca, clasp his elbow – either one will do – with but medium pressure. He will scream like a woman.'

Then he demonstrated the technique. It works best against a fist strike but any extended arm is a satisfactory target. It is not a three part 'get into' lock either but rather an *atemi* directed against the elbow with both open hands simultaneously. If the opponent strikes with his right fist at your body, you cup his elbow upwards from underneath with your left hand opened, and, at the same time, lever down on his wrist with your right hand, palm down. Both thumbs are extended for more surface area. While the leverage is better if your left foot is extended, the trick works well whichever foot is forward. The main thing is to focus exactly and to move both hands in concert. If the opponent strikes with his left, you simply reverse the procedure.

A modification of this 'up and down' method is necessary if the opponent strikes higher, towards your head. Then (if he is using his right) your left hand snaps horizontally inwards and your right hand levers horizontally outwards.

Practise this regularly. Get it in one crisp motion. Work for speed and placement – the power will come later. And actually, if synchronized, very little power is necessary. Above all, be careful with your partner. Keep it very light and save the power for a round post, four inches in diameter, you can nail up.

The elbow is just not designed to withstand this *atemi* of opposite forces which converges cleanly on it in a fraction of a second. I make it a method second to none.

14
THE PATAGONIAN PURR-KICK

*'There's not a foot can swing a boot
Like this here foot of mine'*
Negro Folk Song

IN old Wales there was a favourite pastime called 'purring'. Purring was a quaint form of playful mayhem in which two men wearing heavy shoes faced each other, both hands on the other's shoulders. At the referee's signal, they would begin kicking alternately using both feet on the opponent's shins. And if you think this is outlandish, try pronouncing the name of this Welsh town: Brycheiniog.

It was in Brycheiniog in 1947 that I got a lead on an oldster who was reputed to have been one of the hardiest of the foot stompers. But I kept losing the trail. After three weeks of unavailing search, I was disappointed to learn that my quarry, one J. R. Williams, had but three months previously emigrated to South America.

Apparently he had gone into the restaurant business in Punta Arenas. I wrote him a letter asking for an interview if and when I got to his neighbourhood. J. R. Williams was prompt, if a mite laconic. His return card said simply, 'Come on, sonny.'

I kept the card and as I moved around I often thought of this man. And I wondered what manner of

man it was who would partake of such pain. And I remembered those hackneyed lines from *Hudibras*:
'Some have been beaten till they know what wood a
cudgel's of by th' blow; some kicked until they can
feel whether a shoe be Spanish or neats-leather.'

Along the way I met some fine kickers, chiefly in
China, Japan and India. Men who, unlike an ostrich
(which can only kick forwards), could kick in any
direction with speed and awesome power. There were
some, too, who could and would demonstrate how
they could withstand any kick. I broke my right foot
on one such in Kunming, China. But none of these
ever opposed a shod foot. It was always barefoot you
attacked them. I don't know, they may have been able
to, but I never had the nerve to suggest this test (although I suggested others every bit as nefarious).

Two years after missing him in Wales, I was sitting
with J. R. Williams in his medium-sized and very clean
restaurant in Punta Arenas. It was early afternoon, just
after the luncheon rush, and we sat at a table in the
spacious kitchen. Williams was around sixty, wore a
real healthy glow, and talked mostly in robust exple-
tives. His talk was so salty, in fact, that I make no effort
here to reproduce anything but its substance.

He described the old sport of purring in detail. It
was so widespread at one time, he said, that it was
commonly stated that the strongest legs in the world
belonged to the Welsh. The sport, however, was never
conducted through tournaments but, instead, through
challenge matches and 'friendly' family bouts.

A match could last from two seconds to thirty
minutes. There are reports of matches going for several
hours, but Williams dismissed these as exaggerations.
No padding of any kind was permitted around the leg
and only ordinary work shoes – without steel toes or

J. R. Williams and his speciality

other elaborate reinforcement – were permitted.
Weight was important: the bigger you were the more
power you could get into your kicks. But weight alone
was no guarantee of success. Little men there were
(Williams himself never scaled over 170 pounds) who
could compete with the big ones.

They could do it because the sport was not entirely bereft of skill and technique. Most talented champions would use 'pattern' kicks. Instead of arbitrarily chopping away at the opponent's legs, you kicked a predetermined pattern during which the pain became so unbearable the opponent dropped his arms and stepped away. Of course there were almost as many patterns as there were players. Some used circular patterns, others linear or zig-zag patterns.

Williams used a circular method. First he kicked in the middle of the selected pattern. On his next turn he would kick at twelve o'clock about six inches directly above the centre. Next he would go to three o'clock, then six o'clock, etc, rounding the circle with his vicious kicks. Once around the circle he would tighten it by placing his subsequent kicks slightly closer to the centre than those of the first round had been. Around he would go again. Then an even tighter circle, and so on until he was banging away at the very centre again.

Since you used each foot alternately, both your left and right kicks had to be equally powerful or the advantage would shift to your opponent. Say you had an extremely strong right kick but a modest left one. An opponent with just average right and left kicks would have a good chance against you then because of the weakness of your left foot. Therefore both feet had to be developed as kicking weapons.

And both legs had to be developed to cope with these weapons. This was done through squatting, 'duck-walking', and banging the legs against hard surfaces. But mainly it was done by being kicked. In this sport you really ate bitterness. The pain was intense, especially as the patterns converged on the focal point. Beginners were so abused during kicking practice that, walking home, they screamed if their legs brushed lightly against a bush or another person.

Irrespective of whether you think birds of this feather were plumb loco, you must agree that what kept a man's arms up and his feet kicking could not have been stupidity. After all, stupid people are no more immune to pain than others. No, what kept 'em in there was the same ingredient that you see in all the fighting arts – courage. Papa's definition, 'courage is grace under stress', is as good as any and better than most in this respect.

In purring you had to have courage, guts, spirit, or you would be taken out. In most combat sports, Williams pointed out, you could avoid punishment by skill. There was always a question of Benny Leonard or Young Griffo and the like having guts because these artists were so crafty that they didn't get their hair mussed. Williams asked, if they had been hit would they have been able to stand and fight back? This question never arose in purring because in this art no amount of skill spared you from punishment.

The nature of the game was that if you participated you were punished. Skill really had little to do with it. You needed strong legs and a brave heart to stay in and you needed two good kicking weapons to take your man out. The patterns were the only door that skill walked through and Williams believed that patterns would help little if you were derelict in the other desiderata. The point Williams wanted to make here was simply this: there have been successful boxers who were cowards, but there was never a successful purrer who lacked guts.

As he spoke, the doughty little warrior demonstrated. He moved with a lithe grace and when he raised a leg it was in a crisp powerful movement which indicated a long education.

I next asked him what application purring had for self defence. He laughed and grunted: 'You ever been kicked in the leg?' But he understood me all right. Both of us knew that purring in its standard stereo-typed sameness without modification was a splendid self defence system. But I meant, had he ever modified purring for use in self defence? And he understood.

He had. The deficiency of purring in street fighting, he explained, was that a man with strong legs might withstand the initial kicking onslaught and, with-standing it, deal the attacker a telling counter. You needed a more sensitive target than the leg, and it was logical for Williams to settle on the knee.

The knee is an excellent target. There is always at least one in place, thanks to gravity. A knee cannot have the mobility of the head; if a man chooses to stand, then the knee must put down its roots. If the knee is kept solidly perpendicular to the ground, it can be chipped or broken quite easily with a direct rising kick such as is used in purring. Or, to avoid such an attack, if your opponent withdraws his waist thus straightening the front knee, it's easy to snap it by using the same kick. Anatomically, what goes first of course is the kneecap. So you can see that in any posi-tion the knee can be had.

Since many boxers retain most of their weight on their rear leg it is often necessary to bypass the lead leg and go through with an attack to the rear knee. This is so because kicking a knee which bears no weight is fairly fruitless. Generally, the more weight on the leg, the more damage you can do the knee.

Williams showed me this and more. He felt – with good reason I think – that the direct kick is the quickest, most powerful, and hardest to block. Merely on the point of power, it is four times as powerful as

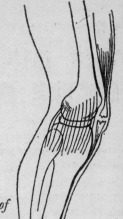

*Cross section of knee showing effects of
Purr-kick*

the lateral thrusts, roundhouses, etc, of some other
systems. Nor did he feel it necessary to snap or thrust
this kick from the standard knee-to-chest position as
taught in *karate*. You swung it up knee straight from
the ground, and only the heel made contact on the
opponent's leg. The *karate* style he felt lost the rising
power and slowed the kick by first insisting that you
bring knee to chest.

He had a standing challenge to anyone in the world
– I was to pass it along – for a kicking match. If fear
stopped them and they wanted a 'no contact' match,
that was fine too he said: he had a stop watch and a
device that measured the power generated on a given
kick. As he said these words he looked at me, obviously
hoping I'd take up the challenge.

Any takers? J. R. Williams of Punta Arenas, kicker
par excellence. I'll tell you how he impressed me. I'm
twenty years younger, fifty pounds heavier, and five-
dan in *karate*. And you know what I told him? I told
him I'd pass the word along!

15
THE DINKY
LITTLE POKE

'Let us be resolute in prosecuting our ends, and mild in our methods of so doing' – *Aquaviva*

ABOUT here the reader might properly ask: 'What about American self defence experts? Don't we have any?'

Not many.

One reason for this is that America has given so many fine boxers to the world. Paradoxical this may sound. I hear the reader ask: 'Isn't boxing self defence?' It is, but – and the but is a big one – it is limited self defence. It knows too many restrictions.* Boxing has been so popular with us that we have all tended to 'play the game' in our street fighting. You know what

---

* I can document this beautifully. A few years ago I spoke with the former middleweight champion of the world. He had been a bearcat in the ring but he knew that outside of it other tactics had to be used. In Hollywood, after his ring career finished, he had been a stuntman. And, like Dempsey, he always had the might-have-beens challenging and teasing him. One such used to follow the champ hoping to goad him into fighting. This guy had the street look about him: big, rough, mean. And the boxer tried to avoid him. But one night the embarrassment was too great and they walked outside. Did the boxer stab and jab and work his ring sequences? Let him tell it.

'We squared off. I feinted with my left; up came his right. I feinted with my right; up came his left. Then I kicked him in the groin. End of battle.'

I mean – the groin is not for hitting; feet are to stand on; no striking below the belt; no elbows, reverses, rabbits, pivots, etc, etc.

And this you cannot do – you can't play the game in the street. It is either him or you. Make your mind up to this fact. Charity may begin at home but on the day you go into the street, leave it there.

Of course there are countless American 'knife and gunners' (a term I use for the half-wits who dare to teach that taking a knife or gun away from a man is easy), but authentic artists are rare. Your best bet for tuition is from accredited (Judo Black Belt Federation) judo gyms.

Currently there is a *karate* craze on in America. Next it will be *aikido*. Charlatans and counterfeits of every description will get into the field just like they did a decade ago with judo. Only in judo they could be challenged and squashed. But with *karate* they can make two years spent in an NCO club in Japan into a fifth degree black belt – and get by with it because the sport is 'too lethal' to contest. I love to tell my Japanese friends that the Chinese and Indians contest it with no resulting casualties: why don't they?

Another thing – there are no rigid grade standards in *karate*. There is a profusion of schools, associations, and independent teachers. So the best advice I can give the reader wanting instruction is this: ask a qualified judo instructor to recommend a *karate* instructor. These boys are usually in the know. Never, repeat *never*, accept a man on his self-announced grade – it may have been self-given (if over second degree black belt, it almost certainly was). It is far better to ask how long he studied under an Oriental instructor in the Far East. If under five years, put it down in your book that he is still a novice.

However, there are some experts who defy classification into a system. Some of them live in the US. One, Bill Seeley, I ran into in Peoria, Illinois, in 1945. The more puritan will be happy to learn that I encountered Bill not in a tavern but in a library.

I was visiting an aunt there for a few weeks, a family obligation, and not enjoying it. So, to use the time with some profit, I was researching Tibetan literature in translation, trying to get a line on ancient self defence in the rarefied climes. I had developed some good leads but the volume I needed (a non-loan book) was being monopolized by a slender, bespectacled chap who had the appearance of not only living in the library, but having been born in the stacks. I surmised that he was on a religious binge and, having conquered yoga, had stormed into the mysteries of lamaism.

I tried to be patient. I waited. But time grew short and I finally interrupted him to request a one day loan. He surprised me by obliging cheerily. After all the waiting, however, I was disappointed. Other than some vague references to a strike targeted on the chin, the book had absolutely nothing of value for me. The following day I returned it to him with the friendly remark that he could now go back to his Buddhism.

'Oh,' he said, 'I have no interest in Buddhism.'

I asked him why he was reading the book.

'It has some excellent material on fighting,' he said, and I was almost floored.

'But that is what I was looking for, and failed to find.'

Smiling he said, 'You are like one who knows a tune but cannot sing. Perhaps it is there, but either your eyes do not see, or, seeing, your brain does not comprehend.'

This wasn't easy to take but he said it in such an

endearing way that I took it. I asked him point-blank to show me the parts that interested him. And so he showed me those vague references.

'But,' I objected, 'these sections say little and what they do say amounts to nothing more than a simple punch on the button. That's pretty standard stuff to come out of mysterious Tibet.'

'Here,' he said pushing the large volume in front of me and pointing, 'read this.'

This is what I read: 'To fight with another is wrong but to lose a fight with another over principles you deem honourable is worse. To fight well is as proper as to study correctly or walk properly. For by learning to fight you actually educate yourself in the avoidance of battle. Technically, most fighting is a complex set of moves and counter moves. However, correct fighting is far simpler. The energy within the abdomen is generated and transmitted via speedy arms centrally to the adversary's chin, whence it causes a reaction within his skull. This is as much knowledge on this point as any diligent student requires.'

That was all. It said no more save for scattered references to 'blows on the chin'. Can you wonder why I was disappointed?

Bill saw I was dissatisfied without my telling him so. He suggested we talk further outside the tomb-like restrictions of the library. In the same breath he introduced himself in the offhand manner at which we Americans are so good.

I agreed and out we went to a small tavern two blocks away. There, seated together and eating ham salad sandwiches and drinking bock beer, he began his narration.

'I have read that volume many times, not just once. Always on the chance that I will find some hint or clue to add to what it has already taught me. But I am afraid the passage you just saw contains the entire content of the fighting instruction of that unknown Tibetan fighter, for I have found nothing more.

'This is not to say I am disappointed. Far from it. For this passage is fairly comprehensive. Granted, it is brief, but the things it says suggest other things which, added to it, make up a system of self defence second to none. The implicit governs when reading Tibetan literature. Remember this. One word may have as much meaning as a hundred words in an American text.'

He then produced a sheet of paper and placed it on the table. The passage had been typed on it.

'I knew you would be disappointed with the excerpt. I was also the first few times. Until I started analysing it. Would you like to hear that it says to me?'

I told him I certainly would.

'All right. In the first sentence a moral case is made against fighting. This is not unique. But then in the same sentence are the words ". . . but to lose a fight with another over principles you deem honourable is worse". This states categorically that defeat cannot be countenanced and suggests that the method used to avoid defeat will be drastic and frightfully efficient. Next, the author equates fighting with studying and walking. I infer this to mean that, like study, fighting requires perseverance, and, like walking, it must become effortless and natural.

'Next, listen to this: "Technically, most fighting is a complex set of moves and counter moves. However, correct fighting is far simpler." Here he tells us that it is not necessary to learn the vast arsenal of offensive and defensive postures and moves which most systems employ.

'Then the author gets to the kernel of the matter. He

The Dinky Little Poke

says that energy is generated from the abdomen. This
energy presumably has to be trained, stored, and chan-
nelled. I interpret that this can be done only by long
practice sessions of deep breathing centred on the
navel. It probably requires concomitant concentration
as well. I expected – and found it to be so – that after a
time this inner power would make itself known in an
unmistakable fashion. I have practised it with some
success for three years.

'The author continues that the power must be trans-

mitted ". . . by speedy arms". This too must be practised rigorously and regularly, but I found that my
arms and hands moved twice as fast as before, solely
through the breathing practice. So, when I added
actual punching exercises, both hands became reflex
fast. Of course I must do better and so I continue with
my daily practice.

'At first I missed the point of "centrally", but when
I found that the punches were not having the effect I
expected, I restudied the passage. I experimented and
found that "centrally" means just that – "centrally".
In other words, the author is saying that the punch
must be delivered from the middle of your body rather
than from the sides so that it strikes your opponent's
chin on a frontally direct line. I first believed the value
in the central strike was because it was shorter. Of
more importance is the fact that your force meets his
chin exactly frontal to it.

'If you strike as a boxer does with crosses, hooks and
jabs you will seldom get the precise fist-to-chin juxta-
position required. Simply because the boxer punches
naturally from either side. That is why you must bring
your fists in towards the mid-point of your body before
punching. Then your fist will move directly on a line
with your chin to meet the point of his chin.

'It is much easier to knock a man out on the chin
than on the jaw. This is what the book says and, surprisingly, it is verified by boxing literature in the West.
E. Jokl's work [1941] is of course the best known. He
established that a knockout is not the result of a nerve
being hit on the chin, paralysis of the functions of the
inner ear, or brain anaemia. Rather, the knockout
occurs in two phases. First, the clivus and the anterior
edge of the occipital bone are pushed against the lower
portions of the pons and the upper anterior surface of

the medulla oblongata. Next, by virtue of the "re-bounding effect", the medulla oblongata bounces back against the internal surface of the occipital bone and the posterior edge of the foramen magnum. In essence, the double impact causes the medulla oblongata, the most sensitive part of the brain, to concuss, thus caus-ing temporary cancellation of the functions of the central nervous system.

'The punch that the Tibetan advocates – really more of a poke – simply tries to ensure the sharpest rebound by making a precisely straight approach squarely on the chin. If it is off-centre, even slightly, the impact on the medulla and its rebounding impact is reduced and unconsciousness is unlikely to ensue. Therefore, the path must be precise.

'So much for theory. Now, what about practice? Let me say in all humility that it works. You can see that my physique was not meant for anything much more arduous than badminton. Yet I have used this poke several times and always with a success so sudden that, if it were done in the ring, the crowd would call it a dive. It was not hard to find opponents. Being the personification of the thin, scrawny scholar, all I have to do is sit in a tavern and invariably the big boys want to lean on me. It's a lesson for them and an education for me. I'm through experimenting. It works and I'm satisfied.'

I asked him then if I could actually witness this poke.

'We may not be able to get a subject,' he said, 'they know me here in Peoria.'

Fools rush in. I volunteered to accept the poke. He was hesitant, reluctant, and my suspicions mounted. But he finally agreed and set the following night as the time. We would meet in the same tavern – called, curiously, the Bluebird – at 8.30 PM. He permitted me

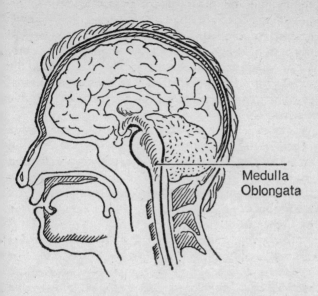

Medulla
Oblongata

Inner view of head showing the sensitive Medulla Oblongata

to pay the bill and, with a tremulous wave, departed.

The next evening at the appointed time I sat in the Bluebird waiting. Time passed as my lips got tighter. It's a story timeless. A person sets his heart on something and, even as he does, half-way knows it will never be. So it was in this instance. Bill Seeley never showed up. That night or the next. Or the next week. I never saw him again.

On my last night in Peoria I paid a last visit to the Bluebird. I asked the bartender the standard question and got the standard negative. He hadn't seen Bill.

But then, it being my last chance, I went further. Did Charlie know where Bill lived? Did he know where Bill worked? He did not. And, as my suspicions knotted into the conclusion that I had been snowed by a real sharpster, Charlie added the words responsible for this chapter being written.

'Sorry mister, I dunno much about him. Keeps his mouth shut when he comes in and doesn't buy enough hootch to make a difference. One thing I can tell you though, he ain't what he looks like. He looks as frail as a pansy. Might even be taken for a limp-wrist. But he ain't, no sir. Believe it or not, that guy's a fighter.'

I was encouraged by this and put in the proper words of astonishment and disbelief. The place was nearly empty; I was alone at the bar. Charlie's narrative was thus relatively uninterrupted.

'Bill had been coming in for some time and we all liked him even though he was pretty quiet. Quiet that is, till the night he had the run-in with the Riddles. I guess every town has its Riddles . . . two brothers who make life hell for decent people. These two were huge oafs. Combined, they probably weighed a quarter of a ton. They had gotten so bad in Peoria that they had been banned by most of the joints, this one included. But that didn't stop them; they went where they wanted and the police actually lived in terror of them.

'Well, this night about six months ago they roll in, full of fire and mean ornery. I put my sap where I could get to it though I realize that if I am forced to use it they'll eat it along with me. So it's just a gesture, you know. They'd fight a bear and give him first bite, those two. They're tough boys.

'It doesn't take them long to size Bill up as a good target. He tried timidly to put them off with words but this made them sore and they really started to lean on him. Jed – the other one was Tom – yanked him up from his chair and I came up with the phone in one hand, the blackjack in the other. Then I saw Jed pitch forward. I had seen no punch so I figured he had stumbled. But he just stayed there, face down on the floor.

'Then Tom grabbed for Bill and this time I saw it, even though by now I was shouting into the phone at the policeman at the other end of the line. Yeah, I saw it. As Tom grabbed him, Bill hit him right on the button, dead on the chin. Funny thing too, it wasn't even a healthy swinging blow. Just a dinky little poke. But it was blur-fast. Anyhow, Tom collapsed on top of Jed and when the riot squad, six strong, came charging in five minutes later, the two of 'em were still asleep.

'The Riddles haven't been in since. But since then I've heard a lot of stories about Bill dumping other characters. I'm not sure what he used on them – maybe the same dinky little poke.'

16
LAST OF THE GREAT
SAVATE MEN

'A pretty foot is one of the greatest gifts of nature'
Goethe

LA boxe française (traditional French boxing) is almost
dead. There are a few schools left in France but the
teachers are starving. The French have turned to the
Japanese martial arts with a vengeance. Traditional
French boxing has been displaced by *karate*.

Guillemin is the last of the orthodox traditionalists
in the sport he calls 'fencing with four limbs'. Even he
may be dead now for, when I last saw him, he was on
the wrong side of eighty.

But this chapter is not of him for he is a traditionalist
in a standardized sport form. Instead this is the story of
Baron J. Fegnier, the last of the great *savate* men, and
his secret methods.

Here it must be pointed out that most foreigners –
especially Americans – erroneously call the classic
sport *savate* rather than French boxing. This is wrong.
French boxing developed from *savate* about 1830. At
that time the hands were incorporated in *savate* foot
fighting into a systematic, regulated sport which fast
became popular. So popular indeed that it killed *savate*.
Or almost did.

As R. W. Smith has said in an excellent study, *savate*
was a vicious type of boxing used chiefly by ruffians in

which the feet were used almost exclusively as attacking members. In *savate* the guard was held low, the
hands open and frontal, and blows were never delivered with the fists. Instead, the open palm was used
to slap the face of the antagonist. *Savate* was so vicious
that the contests held were invariably grudge matches
where honour was at stake. For the most part *savate*
was taught by ruffians to ruffians and the result was
mayhem.

In my sojourn in France I saw considerable of the
waning art of French boxing but I never expected to
see *savate*. Through the agency of a woman (never mind
how) I got on the track of Baron Fegnier who, she had
heard, had a 'funny kind of fighting'.

Like many boxers, the Baron was poor; and money
is meant to be spent. So it was that I was able to see his
exercise for an hour in 1956. It was strange that he
should term this vicious thing an exercise, but he
always did.

Baron Fegnier was sixty-seven when I saw him, a
spry white-haired veteran. He explained initially that
the *savate* he had learned was essentially the same as
that taught by Michel Pisseux in the first quarter of the
nineteenth century, which had been supplanted by
French boxing. French boxing almost killed it. But one
teacher, Lafond, resisted the new sport, continued
teaching *savate*, and it had thus been handed down
through the years to Fegnier. In answer to my question
at this juncture, the Baron stated that since there was
no one 'worthy', he was taking the art to the grave
with him.

Then he went on to berate me for the Americans
who advertised courses in *savate*.

'They know nothing except publicity,' he said.
'They pretend to a skill they do not possess. All one

Fegnier's fearsome High Kicks

has to do is to look at their postures in their terrible books. Even a novice can assume a correct posture – they err when they begin to move. But these Americans cannot even get into a correct posture. Some of these poses look as if the poser had suddenly had an attack of flatulence.'

That out of the way, he showed me his skill. He squatted with knees bent and he came out of this shell with legs flashing in a blur. He glided with knees stiff; he pranced; he whirled. And all the while these moves were punctuated by kicks of the fastest legs I have ever seen. A snake strikes at five miles per hour and a fast boxer at twenty-five miles per hour. I estimated Fegnier's feet at over thirty miles per hour!

He paused and told me that although *savate* concentrated chiefly on low kicks, he had developed the high kick as a special weapon. The nose and the lips he deemed the best target due to their sensitivity.

He acknowledged that the high kick targeted for the head could be dangerous to the attacker, but he sincerely felt that his speed was of such an order that, even if he missed the opponent, he could recover before a counter could be effected.

'This is not braggadocio,' he said. '*Savate* is too dangerous to be competed. But I have fought with it many times against all manner of men in no-quarter-asked-or-given fights. Always I emerged successful. That is why I am so dogmatic.'

He put a ripe tomato in my teeth and asked me to stand on a line opposite him. Then he told me that the moment I detected any movement by him I should withdraw my head or body as quickly as I could.

He faced me, a small smile on his face. I watched his shoulders for a sign. I sensed something and reacted reflexively. But too late – the tomato was all over my

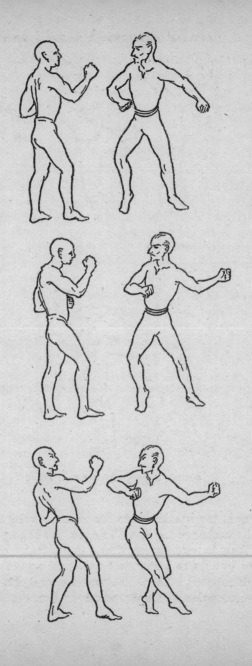

Sequence showing the Baron at his best

face, in my hair and eyes, all except a small portion still clenched by my teeth! The man was like lightning!

Then he told me he would intentionally miss my nose by a fraction of an inch and that I was to counter with anything I liked. This was my meat, the sort of demonstration I sought wherever I met a fighting master. For this is the sort of thing that proves a system.

We squared off. This time I really tried to tune in on him. Then his toes were a blur under my eyes and immediately I put a size twelve right foot in the direction of his scrotum. I kick well and I kick swiftly but it was almost as though he had had time to shower and shave. He brought the right foot with which he had kicked down and thrust his left foot into my incoming tibia. Irresistible force and immovable object, indeed! The force of his left kick did not divert my foot; it stopped it in mid-motion. There was a flash of intense pain and my body weight coming forward rocked, and then I came down on my right knee.

To his insincere, 'Does it hurt!' I retaliated with a wry 'Only when I laugh.' After a brief respite, during which he applied some analgesic balm to my abused member, he picked up where he had left off.

'These foolish *karate* people make so much of breaking brittle bricks and tiles when they should be working on distance appreciation and placement. For, along with speed, these are the keys to fighting skill. Power is strictly secondary. Let me show you what I mean.'

I hobbled to a standing position and again he approached me. Then he began kicking my ear lobes, using both feet alternately. Each kick was a flash and each barely grazed my lobes. There was no pain and I began to enjoy it when suddenly the intensity of force began to increase. It continued, and now the pain was quite severe. Still he kept on and now the lobes had become numb and again I hardly felt the kicks. Then he stopped.

'You thought, like most persons, that the ear lobes are not very sensitive. But even this limited area can be hurt. And how did I hurt you? The kicks were all of equal power. But the first kicks I used were against that part of the lobe furthest from your head. When I brought the kick in against the part closest to your head, then your facial nerves felt pain which was transmitted by the sensory nerves of your cheeks through the upper part of your ear and down again to the lobes. But even this pain was of short duration and the entire ear soon numbed. I merely showed this to indicate that even a small target can be divided.'

Time was running out but I requested a final demonstration. He kindly consented. He lit a cigarette and asked me to puff it several times and then hold it between my lips. I did. He came up to me, looked at the cigarette once intently, and lashed up with his foot.

He had missed! The master hits the dirt. When it happens you talk, apologize for him, blame something you didn't do for the failure, etc, but deep down you know some enjoyment. The infallible falls.

Fegnier hadn't acknowledged the miss however. He just stood and smiled. I don't smoke, but nervously I took a puff on the cigarette.

Have you guessed? I didn't inhale. I couldn't – there was no fire! Baron Fegnier had doused the thing with a foot so controlled that I hadn't felt it. I looked at the cigarette end incredulously while he chuckled.

As we said our farewells his last words were, 'Tell your fighting friends to forget power and work on distance appreciation and placement. Only then will they progress.'

17
THE PEKING
MAN

'I am seeking a man' – Diogenes

PEKING. 1946. The ravages of war everywhere. Peking the picturesque; Peking the grand. Possessing the prettiest girls and the most noxious smells in the world. City of contrasts, city of paradoxes. Peking. 1946.

Chou Hsu-lai was no more than 5 feet 6 inches tall and 140 pounds heavy. Yet he was the man I had been hearing about since 1938. In the far west of China, in Szechwan Province, sterling boxers had said, 'My method may seem to you art – but go to see Chou Hsu-lai. Go to Peking.'

And in Canton, and in Lanchou, and in Mukden, always the same story: 'Go to Peking to see Chou.' Now there are no people so individualistic and proud as the Chinese. Boxers carry the trait to even greater limits than the average Chinese. They seldom speak a word for any other boxer unless it is critical. And that was why this collective and continual advice puzzled and excited me. To get such a consensus, the man Chou must be superlative.*

* One story told of him concerned some rival boxers who attempted to embarrass him by bringing him a trick brick to break: one that had two steel reinforcing rods baked into it. Notwithstanding this, Chou swiped the thing in two with no

But here he was sitting opposite me, smiling rau-
cously and smoking opium. Although many famous
Chinese boxers used opium, this was my first close
contact with the fact. The odour was sickening and
early on I thought to break off cleanly and quickly –
nothing was worth this. But I set my stomach and
endured. It was a blessing I did. He conquers who
endures. This is what Chou told and showed me in the
two hours we had together.

He had boxed since age fourteen when, as a poor
servant in a rich merchant's house, he had secretly
observed the merchant's two sons being put through
their paces by a grizzled boxing veteran. By age
twenty-five he was the best boxer in Shansi, a province
noted for its boxing. *Hsing-i*, *pa-kua*, *t'ai-ch'i*, and
shaolin – he mastered them all. By forty he was one of
the finest masters in all China. In one year he accepted
as many as eighteen challenges and won them all. He
had killed five men in such matches and felt no com-
punction. After all, he told me, he had never challenged
– the onus was on the challenger.

He was then sixty-five and living on funds provided
by several commercial firms which used his name on
the banners of their goods-caravans transiting North
China. His name sufficed to keep bandits at bay. He
had never taught boxing commercially. Indeed, in his
entire career he had had only six students.

One part of his success, he stated, was skill of course.
The other was innovation. Since most boxers learned
the basic moves of the basic schools they in time became trapped by their very technique. Realizing this,
he had modified and added. His new method he called
'Liberation Boxing' because it enabled him to escape

---

discernible effort! The tricksters vacated immediately without
picking up the pieces.

the stereotyped formulations of the standard schools.

His principle can be explained thus: some boxers put value on method; others pride themselves on dispensing with method. To be without method is bad, but to depend entirely on method is worse. At first you must learn the fundamentals thoroughly and then modify them according to your ability. The zenith of all method is to seem to have no method.

He never exhibited his wares. He didn't have to. A few boxers had been party to his artistry and the word had spread. His reputation was secure.

Then he showed me a portion of his repertoire. A husky student attacked him in a violent, unrehearsed manner and was repeatedly bounced off the walls for his efforts. The student did not once penetrate the seemingly slow-moving target. Chou observed that if I had watched closely I would have seen that this was no Japanese make-believe *kata* (form). This was China and the attack was real. He asked if I would like to try. Everywhere else when asked and offered some guarantee against serious injury I had accepted. Chou Hsu-lai was another matter. It does not diminish me to admit that I was frightened. I declined. He smiled as one smiles when thinking about the dead.

The body must be protected, he continued, or the opponent will not suffer. Then, taking me to an inner courtyard partially covered with wood near the edges, he asked me to wait. A moment later I heard his voice and looked up to see him standing in a third-storey open window. Enjoining me not to move, he announced that he would jump beside me. The next moment his small body was in flight. The next is incredible. Of course he landed on the wooden surface without injury, but this I had seen Japanese and Thai non-boxers do previously. But Chou landed not only

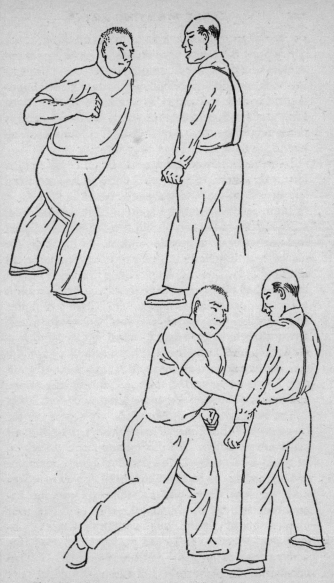

Chou Hsu-lai's pupil using Ch'i to withstand a punch

without injury but also without sound! I swear it – I saw it but I did not hear it. A physicist may be able to explain it. I own that I cannot.

Shunting aside my flabbergasted words of amazement, he next asked me to lift him. Now Johnny Coulon, the former bantam boxing champ, does much the same feat of resisting a lift. Only Johnny uses his hands lightly for leverage to impede the lifter. Chou did not; he kept his hands at his sides. I could not lift him even a little. First I tried both hands under his armpits. Then the left on his breastbone and the right through his legs and clasping his belt in the rear. Nothing worked. Then his stocky student stood with me and we tried together. And we tried. Complete failure. Through all this Chou stood slumped and relaxed.

This is all very well, Chou then observed, but you will doubtless meet people who will tell you that I hypnotized or rapported you. So, as a final test, he asked me to forget what I had just seen, generate hatred for him and square off with him: I to use any style I liked. He solaced me by saying he would not touch me. I chose an orthodox Western boxing stance with the left fist extended and advanced on him. I was determined not to go off-balance or to let him turn either corner. Then we were in close. His right hand flashed inside my left and – forgetting his promise not to touch me – I moved my left slightly to deflect it. Then – then he was not there! I heard him chuckle and turning, found him smiling *behind* me. Don't ask me how he got there. I'm blessed if I know. I tried again, three times more in fact, and each time *he went behind me without my visual detection of it!*

All this happened over fifteen years ago. Things have changed in China since. Possibly Chou Hsu-lai is no longer alive, I don't know. But I do know that he made me believe those words of *Genesis*: 'There were giants in the earth in those days.' I believe because, you see, I met one.

18
MÉLANGE OF MAYHEM

' My fellow-servant Umphry Klinker bid him be sivil,
and he gave the young man a douse in the chops;
*   but . . . Mr Klinker wasn't long in his debt – with*
*   a good oaken sapling he dusted his doublet'*
T. G. Smollett

THIS chapter is a potpourri. Here I make a brief
catalogue of persons and methods in the self defence
realm interesting but not profound.

Every book should have a girl, if not a heroine. Stella
Bisbey is all I have in this line. Four years senior to me
in the school system of a small California town in the
1930s, Stella was as poor as a church mouse and as
tough as a mongoose. She had to be, for a day without
a screaming, scratching girl fight in that school didn't
occur often. By her junior year, Stella was girl champ
of the school and even the boys gave her wide berth. I
can remember what was virtually her only technique.
She would first slap a blinder into her opponent's eyes
to confuse, and immediately step in, take two five-
fingered handfuls of hair, and pivoting, pull forward
like hell. It was either surrender or be scalped and most
opted for the former. The real toughies who would
fingernail you to death even as you pulled out their

hair, Stella dealt with differently. Here she modified by extending the technique into a near relative of *tai-otoshi* (judo body drop – a hand throw in which you pivot so that your body is aligned in the same direction as your opponent's, your foot blocking the outside of his ankle). Flipping them over the foot she then kicked them in the short ribs. Stella was perhaps not a lady, but every bit a champion.

Slim Moyer of Wichita also used a variant of *tai-otoshi* with what he described as good results. He even called it *tie-otoshi*. You guessed it. In man-fights he didn't have the hair to adhere to so he would grab the chap's necktie and bring him over that way. I asked him what he'd use if the antagonist were, like Harry Truman, a bow-tie fan. He responded that then he'd attack by stabbing inwards to the throat with the collar stays in the man's shirt. He said this with a steady eye, but I don't know. It smacks strongly of the Wrist Watch Winding Stem Restraint which a New Zealander once swore certain rowdies put to nefarious use in Wellington. They allegedly would snatch the stem of an expensive watch and ask the victim blithely for $5,00 (or its equivalent in the local currency) for a 'spot of tea'. The victim would be apt to comply, fearing the breaking of the stem. Presumably this would not work on self-winding watches. A last entry under this head: in 1942 the soldiers at Camp Ellis, Illinois, used to use the following tactic. They would approach a buddy and with the left hand reach under his right blouse lapel and yank off the base cap of his insignia. Then, with the base of the right palm they would bang down on the insignia, drilling the shaft into his chest. The shaft was too short to bring blood but it brought bruises, curses, and general hilarity.

*   *   *

You may know Juneau and if you do, you might know
Don Eagle. Bartender, cook, general dog-robber, Don
is pretty good in the street. Actually, he was smarter
than he was tough. In those icy Alaskan streets he won
a helluva reputation using primarily one technique.
Don would manoeuvre his antagonist on to ice and
would try at the same time to get at least one of his
own feet on stable ground. He called this phase the
'sale' and he accomplished it by a talkative spiel. When
he had his bird on ice, Don would fake with his hands,
shift his weight to the stable foot, and sweep his
opponent's legs. A sweep on ice. The boys really went
flying, even the Kodokan crew would have been en-
vious. Another thing Don was good at: he bested
every Eskimo hardhead in the time-honoured 'sport'
of head bashing. Since time began the Eskimos have
played at this sport which consists of one man grab-
bing another by the scruff of the neck and hammering
his head backwards into the side of an igloo. Then it's
the other chap's turn. The first one to break the foot-
thick, ice-encrusted snow brick of the igloo won.
Occasionally a man's head gave out before the bricks
did. I had it on good authority that Don – half-Eskimo
himself – had beaten the best the Eskimos could bring
forward. I know when I asked him about it he thought
in his vacant way that I was challenging him and he
enthusiastically began to lead the way. I had a devil of a
time deterring him. Speaking to the principle of the
thing, Don at least implied that it was not so much the
thrust of your offensive snap which won as it was the
ability of your head to take the concussive battering.
Hence, I can't recommend the method to any save
those with tremendously hard crowns who take delight
in having them battered against igloos.

*   *   *

*Don Eagle with the weightlifter's gambit:
'He went that-a-way'*

And then there were the training room antics having to
do with jock strap flips, zippers, and leaving a man in
a full squat with a barbell weighing 400 pounds on his
shoulders and his 'spotters' called away by an insistent
phone call and never returning. Good clean fun. But
there was nothing clean and nothing funny about Lou
Renton of Chicago. Lou was a street fighter of no
mean quality. Lou insisted that more fights are lost by
feints and meaningless jabs than by anything else. He
preferred the unorthodox method of getting in close
and then spitting a stream of tobacco juice into the
victim's eyes and then following with what he called
'the dirty stuff'. Lou had a hard heart.

19
A MASTER OF KIAI-JUTSU

'Beyond one's powers' – Horace

SHEP LACEY (which was not his real name) was something of a bore. He left his soul unmanned; he lived a half-way sort of life. He dabbled in everything and, for the two years I knew him in Japan in 1950–52, he was a constant problem.

I did the best I could for him. I introduced him to leading judo, *kendo*, *karate* and *aikido* masters and he studied under them for a while. A darned short while. He lacked perseverance, what the Russians call *vynoslivost* ('living a thing out'). And it was too bad, for he possessed a body second to none in muscularity and general athletic tone.

I remember once we were doing *randori* (judo practice) in a small gym. He shuffled and seemed to brood. I implored him to attack me but he just shuffled. After two or three minutes of this he looked directly into my eyes and said soft as a girl, 'John, do you like buttermilk?' That was the kind of a guy he was.

I say this in candour not rancour. For, with all his faults, Shep was gold down deep. I owe him a big debt. Without him the present chapter would not be penned. This is how it was ...

Twilight was coming on in Shibuya. Shep and I had just eaten and were at an intersection waiting for the traffic lights to change. Tokyo traffic in those years certainly wasn't that it is today but, even though the *kamikaze* drivers were fewer, they were still *kamikaze*.

The light turned green and we started across. A snarl of oncoming tyres warned us and we halted to stay clear of the small green taxi speeding through the intersection, oblivious of the lights. A tiny Japanese man beside us stopped too and put out his hand to restrain the young girl with him. But too late; she was already in the middle of the street and did not hear the car bearing down on her. I have excellent reflexes but I stood rooted. The Japanese, we found out later, had even better reflexes but he too was incapable of action.

It was the moment of truth. And Shep Lacey shone. With a spring he was out in the middle of the street, snatched up the girl, and threw himself into a perfect *chugairi* or shoulder roll, the more surprising since he had never stuck long enough with judo to learn this form of falling. The taxi barely missed the flying two and they came up unscathed.

The first thing I said to the smiling Shep when I ran up may have been silly but I meant it.

'Shep,' I said, 'I loathe buttermilk but I like you!'

The little eight-year-old girl, Michiko, was crying softly and the little gentleman was patting her on the shoulders and hugging her. He suggested we repair to a nearby teahouse while we all got our nerves back in trim.

An ice cream curbed the child's tears and the Japanese man, Shep and I sipped tea. His name was Junzo Hirose, a quite affluent practitioner of traditional medicine with a speciality in bonesetting. He may have been fifty or – with Orientals assessing age is precarious indeed – sixty. I mentioned jocosely that for a moment it looked like we might have a couple of patients for him.

'Please,' he said, 'I mean no offence. You Americans love to joke. And I love that quality in you. But what has just happened let us forget for ever.'

He told us then that his wife and a son had been run down two years before and all of his skill in medicine had been unable to repair the damage done by the onslaught of steel.

We commiserated with the appropriate words. He waved us off and very seriously asked what he could do for us to show his gratitude. Shep then waved him off, saying it had been a delightful experience; adding, however, that he wouldn't want to do it again.

We drank more tea. And talked. Shep was always as garrulous as an old woman. And so it was that he mentioned my research into the martial arts. Hirose's eyes took on a new light. I saw and held my breath, the old hopes rising in my breast. He urged Shep to continue and Shep did. Oh how he did. He bragged me up out of all proportion.

Then Hirose asked if I had ever heard of *ninjutsu*, the art of invisibility or camouflage. Indeed I had. *Ninjutsu* was a secret art taught to élite spies before and during Tokugawa times. It taught one to cross rivers on foot by using floats of wood and horsehide; to walk seventy-five miles a day sideways; to scale twenty-foot walls; and to do other seemingly impossible things.

Hirose smiled as I said this, nodded when I finished.

'What you say is true,' he said, 'but have you ever actually seen a *ninja*?'

I sighed and told him that I had not. I had heard that there were a few masters still alive but I had been unable to find any.

I added, 'I would give almost anything to speak with a *ninja*.'

To which he answered, with a bright look at Shep: 'You need not give anything. Mr Lacey has earned you both a demonstration. For you see I am one of the – as you rightly say – few masters still alive. Can you come to this address next Tuesday evening around seven o'clock?' He then gave each of us his name card. Thus the interview ended.

Just like that. You may be sure that at the appointed time we were there taking off our shoes, and entering the confines of a palatial home.

Tea and cookies were brought in by a kimonoed maid. She left and there were only the three of us. Without further preliminaries, Hirose launched into his exposition of *ninjutsu*. He told us of its origin and history: springing before Tokugawa from *samurai* beginnings because of the military necessity and carried to the present by a spirit which rose in wartime, diminished in peacetime, and had largely died since gunpowder and modern weaponry had been introduced. Fairly rapidly he skimmed its philosophic ethic which, unsurprisingly, was bound up with Buddhism/Taoism.

Then he moved into its rationale. A *ninja*, he said, had to be able to walk further and faster, jump higher, fight better, hide easier, and escape quicker than other *samurai*. The training was more painful than anything in the world. For years you spent almost every minute in hardening and preparing your body.

He asked me to put torsion on his wrist. I got an effective lock and began heavy pressure. With a snap he dislocated his own wrist. I still held it but it was like holding a limp dishcloth. You cannot dislocate a wrist if it's already dislocated! He did the same thing with

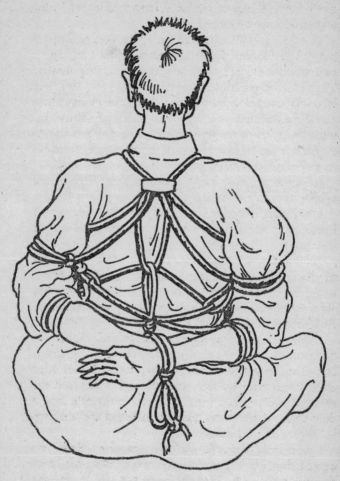

The tie which failed on Junzo Hirose

his elbow and shoulder. And, to make it complete, he did it with his knee and ankle. In short, here was a man who could not be locked.

Then he asked to be tied up. This was an opportunity I had longed for. Some years before I had spent two weeks in Chengtu, China, with a roping master. That old codger could escape anything you tied him into and could also truss you up so securely that all you could move were your eyeballs. I roped Hirose up with one of these methods in which, if you attempt to extricate a leg or move an arm, you strangle yourself. In thirty seconds Hirose was out, smiling.

And yet he paid me a compliment. 'Where,' he asked, 'did you learn that tie?'

I told him. He nodded and said that it was very good. Presumably anything less he could have been out of instantly!

He asked me to put a rear choke on him. This was too much! In the *shime-waza* (strangling arts) of judo I stood supreme. There were perhaps two or three Japanese who offered me competition on this score. But Hirose had asked for it.

I dug in on *hadaka-jime* and he wilted. Again the dishcloth analogy was apropos. I persisted in my choke, however, even against the limp posture he afforded until I was sure he was unconscious. I released my strangle and stepped back to let his body fall. But it didn't fall. It, he, stood. He was standing and smiling.

'Is that all?' he asked.

I was truly shocked on this one. He offered no explanation, but immediately went into his next demonstration. A brawny assistant in a *hakama* sauntered in with a piece of wood (approximately eighteen inches long, six inches wide, and four inches thick) and a Japanese sword. The assistant and Shep held the wood while Hirose lined up on it and in one searing slicing motion went through it with the sword.

Handing the sword to his assistant, he turned towards me. 'That was merely to show you the sharpness of the sword, not my ability with it – for really I have none. Please watch carefully now. By concentration I will isolate various components of my body so that a sharp sword will not penetrate the skin.'

He stood there solemn now but quite relaxed. His assistant stood near with the sword poised. Finally, Hirose indicated the right bicep with his left index finger. The assistant took the sword and placed the edge against the master's right bicep and then, with a small grunt, bore down with his weight on it. Hirose stood, arm outstretched, while his assistant laboured. To no avail. The skin was not broken and no blood seeped. I looked at his arm. There was only a slight red line caused by pressure of the blade.

'Have you practised *kendo*?' he asked.

When I told him I was only Second Grade Black Belt in the sport, he laughed, 'That is certainly enough to know how to swing a sword.' Then he asked me to strike *with all my strength* at his left forearm. He enjoined me to focus well since, if I hit his upper arm inadvertently, it would be unfortunate.

I took the sword from the assistant, focused on Hirose's arm, and brought the sword down sharply. I could exaggerate and say I used all my strength. In truth, I did not. I was afraid that if I used everything my focus might be disturbed and I might hit his upper arm. So I used controlled power but certainly enough to have sliced through the wood like he had done.

No half-arm fell on the floor. No blood spurted. Hirose did not scream or faint. In an unbelieving trance I held his arm and gazed at it. A red line creased the skin, but that was all. The master gestured us to be seated again.

'I will not pretend that what you have just seen is not artistry. It is. Few indeed are those who can do it. But I must own to some regret about it. For no one has ever been able to isolate the entire body from attack – only components. So you see it is of limited value. In a duel I could hardly ask my antagonist to confine his strikes to only this or that part of my body.'

Seating himself on the *tatami* he said, 'There is a complete method, however, of which I am a master and about which I have no regrets. Shall I demonstrate?'

To my hurried affirmative, he began.

'This system is rarer even than *ninjutsu*. It is called *kiai-jutsu*. Have you heard of it?'

I said I had but that I understood it was superhuman and legendary, subject not at all to scientific research.

'No,' he responded, 'not superhuman. Say rather supernormal. There is so much in the martial arts which requires only concerted practice to yank it from an ethereal status to a more mundane one. *Kiai-jutsu* (spirit shout art), though rare, has not been the exclusive province of Japanese. I suppose many Chinese had the ability and did not the Trojan, Hector, have a ferocious shout? Also, I have heard that the ancient Irish warriors used a hero shout which could drive armies backwards. Speaking of legend, in the woods of old Greece there were shouts which would make hardy men quake, quiver, and in the end reduce them to jellied masses. These shouts were attributed to the god Pan and I understand that this legend is the father of the word "panic" in your language.

'But to return. *Kiai-jutsu* is not superhuman. It does, however, require an innate talent. Some men have the talent and never realize it sufficiently to develop it. I knew a Buddhist priest once who walked into a stable seeking road directions. He had not said five words when the entire structure came down on him. You see, his voice was exactly attuned or geared to that building. This sort of thing happened so often to the poor man that he was obliged to speak in whispers the rest of his life to avoid embarrassing incidents.

'If you doubt the physics of this art, put a violin and a drinking glass together and, when the violin plays its note, the glass will shatter. Caruso could do it with his wonderful voice. In the field of subsonics and supersonics scientists now can make sound cool, heat, and cut. Why not kill? *Kiai-jutsu* is a matter of tone, vibration, articulation, and – most important – spirit or will. But here, I promised to demonstrate, not lecture you to ennui.'

At this point he gestured to his assistant who rose and came near him. Hirose then slapped him sharply across the face and immediately a rivulet of crimson came from the man's nose. It came steadily for perhaps fifteen seconds and then I was positively jangled by a force which seemed to come from underneath the house. Then it was gone like a clap of thunder. My eyes darted from the master to his assistant. The blood had stopped coincident with the *kiai*.

'I said earlier that I had no regrets about this art. I meant it. It is the perfect fighting art. For in a street fight the best fighter in the world can be killed accidentally. And, purposely or accidentally, what difference does it make if you are dead?

'*Kiai-jutsu* permits no accidents. It can kill or wound from a distance, a distance the opponent cannot employ to his advantage or helpful accident.

'Now it is getting quite late and we have time for

only one more demonstration. Would you care to be my partner in this?'

Not too avidly I consented.

'Good. You are about ten feet from me. Mr Lacey will be so good as to count to three slowly. On three you must stand and attack me.'

Shep started the count. By now the evening's activities had taken a terrible toll on my emotions and I was fairly flustered. But when I heard three intoned I started up, intent on the attack.

But a moment later I still sat there. I reasoned that Shep had not yet said three. I had not heard anything. Or experienced anything. Yet, something *had* happened. For Hirose and his assistant were standing and speaking in low tones. My mind was very fuzzy. I turned to Shep and he was laughing idiotically.

'Stop laughing and say three,' I demanded.

At this he laughed even harder. Then he stopped and said: 'Dammit John, I said it.'

'But he didn't shout,' I blurted.

Shep rejoined: 'He shouted man, my, how he shouted!'

20
ICELANDIC
POSTSCRIPT

'So fight I, not as one that beateth the air'
I Corinthians 9 :26

AND now I'm in Iceland, home of the world's most
intellectual race and of that fascinating wrestling form
Glima ('flash'). I had meant to stay only two months
and I have been here six already. Why? Now that is a
story.

The second week I was here in Reykjavik it happened. I saw a friend off at the railway station and after
his train left I walked down the platform, preparing to
exit from the depot. But an altercation developed at the
ticket office. A large, well-set-up gent was pushing a
medium-built blond fellow with short, jerking pushes
which usually infuriate a man into swinging. They
barred my way, so I stopped to watch (if you have
come this far there's not a reader who would think that
I wouldn't have stopped even if they hadn't blocked
me).

Finally the blond did what the goading bull wanted;
he swung. But coincident with his swing a policeman,
who had approached without our knowledge, pushed
him slightly, thus deflecting the punch. It struck the
big one's shoulder glancingly and boomed into a steel
stanchion. Then the policeman grabbed them both and

hustled them away. It seemed to me that the big fellow's eyes had a wondering look and his shoulder a pronounced list as he was marched off.

Then I did what I shouldn't have (otherwise I'd be in America now). I looked at the huge steel stanchion. And what I saw made my eyes pop. The impress of the blond chap's fist was clearly and unmistakably engraved in the steel to a depth of a full quarter inch! The stanchion was not of deficient steel. Fool that I am, I tested it (my hand is still numb) and no posterity will see my mark because it isn't there. What manner of man must this be? To have a punch, partially deflected by a push and a shoulder, dig into steel. Truly incredible. I had to find the man.

The police bureau laughed at my inquiries. They disowned knowledge of the incident. No one had either entered the hospitals here or been treated for a broken hand by any doctor in the city. I checked this out thoroughly. So I continue the search for the man with the incredible punch. One day, maybe tomorrow, I'll find him and – perhaps – begin another book . . .

ABOUT THE AUTHOR

' Enter boldly, for here also there are Gods' – *Heraclitus*

As publishers, we feel this book should end with a short history of the author. All too frequently books on fighting arts are written by persons who have nothing more than a vague understanding of the subject matter of which they write. The reading public has the right to know the facts about any author. Here they are.

The author, John F. Gilbey, is one of the last of the giants. Like those he writes about he is a master of fighting. Heir to a textile fortune, he was able from an early age to begin a systematic education of his body. He now knows self defence like no other man alive: a seven-*dan* in judo (Yamamoto method: the highest graded Caucasian in the world); five-*dan karate*; holder of a master's certificate in Chinese boxing – the only Westerner to be so accredited; and victor over A. Diaz, Brazilian *capoeiragem* champion in a pitched battle in 1954 which saw both the victor and the vanquished go to a hospital afterwards. He is also a scholar, fluent in seven languages, and holder of a PhD.

A remarkable man. How did he achieve it? By work; sheer hard work. Frankly, Mr Gilbey was not keen about our publishing his work. For several years we urged publication. He relented only when it appeared that new fighting sports such as judo, *karate* and *aikido* were gaining enough popularity for him to comment

The author, John F. Gilbey

on them, comparing them to other more secret methods.

Besides being perhaps the ablest all-round fighter in the world today, the author is a superb stylist who makes the men and their violent specialities in this book march before your eyes. As graphic reportage this is without peer; as instruction in systematic self defence it will perhaps never be equalled. We commend it unreservedly to the public.

Ian Fleming

The Man with the Golden Gun   40p

James Bond 'twisted like a dying animal on the ground and the iron in his hand cracked viciously ...'

'Pistols' Scaramga

Professional assassin for KGB and other criminal organizations. A paranoiac and sexual fetishist, he used a gold-plated Colt with silver bullets to avenge himself upon humanity.

Mary Goodnight

'A naked arm smelling of Chanel No 5 snaked round Bond's neck, and warm lips kissed the corner of his mouth.'

'Fleming keeps you riveted' *Sunday Telegraph*

'Some of the best ingredients of the Bond sagas'
Bristol Evening Post